The Black Book

The Black Book

Woodrow Wilson's
Secret Plan for Peace

Wesley J. Reisser

LEXINGTON BOOKS
Lanham • Boulder • New York • Toronto • Plymouth, UK

Published by Lexington Books
A wholly owned subsidary of The Rowman & Littlefield Publishing
Group, Inc.
4501 Forbes Boulevard, Suite 200, Lanham, Maryland 20706
www.rowman.com

10 Thornbury Road, Plymouth PL6 7PY, United Kingdom

British Library Cataloguing in Publication Information Available

Library of Congress Cataloging-in-Publication Data
Reisser, Wesley J.
  The black book : Woodrow Wilson's secret plan for peace / Wesley J.
Reisser.
     p. cm.
  Includes bibliographical references.
  ISBN 978-0-7391-7111-0 (cloth : alk. paper) — ISBN 978-0-7391-7112-7
(electronic)
  1. World War, 1914–1918—Territorial questions. 2. World War, 1914-
1918—Peace. 3. Paris Peace Conference (1919-1920) 4. Europe—
Boundaries—History—20th century. 5. Middle East—Boundaries—
History—20th century. 6. Wilson, Woodrow, 1856-1924. I. Title.
  D650.T4R45 2012
  940.3'12—dc23
                                                        2011053461

For my parents, Kurt and Susan Reisser,
and in memory of my grandmother, Kathryn Reisser,
who started teaching me about President Wilson and
World War I as a small child.

Contents

Acknowledgments

Without the assistance and mentorship of many people, I would not have been able to undertake this project successfully, and to them I am deeply grateful. I would like to acknowledge Dr. Marie Price for her advice, mentoring and inspiring my interest in World War I and its consequences, and especially for her introducing me to the work of Dr. Isaiah Bowman while an undergraduate at the George Washington University. I also extend special thanks to Dr. John Agnew of UCLA for his continued encouragement and the constant bouncing of ideas with me that has dramatically shaped how I see the world and vastly expanded my knowledge of geography. The other members of my doctoral committee at UCLA, Dr. Michael Curry, Dr. Nicholas Entrikin, and Dr. Ivan Berend, have also provided me with stellar support throughout this project. Several colleagues within the UCLA Geography Department, including Tristan Sturm, Scott Stephenson, Erin Streff, Jennifer Goldstein, Vena Chu, amongst others also deserve thanks for their encouragement and willingness to bounce around many of the ideas I have pursued in this work. I would like to thank Joe Dymond at the George Washington University for his assistance in editing and research of my masters, of which this project was a major extension. I also want to acknowledge my mother, Susan Reisser, and Jacob Palley, for their tremendous assistance in the editing of my work.

Two research libraries and their staffs have also been extremely important in this effort. The Ralph Bunche Library at the U.S. Department of State has provided me with incredible original materials, including original maps from the Paris Peace Conference that they made available to me. Reference librarian Linda Schweizer was especially helpful in aiding my tracking down of resources at the Department. I could not have done my work without the use of the Isaiah Bowman Manuscripts at the Milton S. Eisenhower Library at Johns Hopkins University. The help of their staff, especially Margaret Burri, Curator of Manuscripts, made it possible for me to use the original manuscript copy of the Inquiry's Black Book and maps in order to construct the original American plan for peace in 1919.

And last but certainly not least, I want to thank those that assisted me in the cartographic work of my project: Nuala Cowan, the Spatial Analysis Manager at the George Washington University, and Vena Chu and Scott Stephenson at UCLA. Their incredible help and proficiency with GIS allowed me to create new maps based on historic sources used in this work.

CHAPTER 1

The Inquiry & the 1919 Paris Peace Conference

In the closing days of 1917, the United States entered the "War to End All Wars," the First World War. For over four years, European states had been locked in a struggle that eventually left almost ten million soldiers and countless civilians dead, thus making it the single largest war to date ever fought.[1] As the war broke out, most European leaders remained blind to what they were embarking upon, making the assumption that the war would be short and that the European system could weather this storm and remain on top.[2] The United States had never before entered a European conflict, only playing a role in such wars when they came to North America, such as the War of 1812. The United States prided itself in avoiding the intrigues of the imperial powers and pursuing an independent course. With entry in World War I, the era of American isolationism came to an abrupt end.

A host of issues led to the conflict. The most widely accepted view is that World War I broke out for structural reasons, an argument centered on the idea that any disturbance in the European balance of power would tip the system off kilter.[3] The assassination of Austro-Hungarian Archduke Ferdinand did exactly that, leading to a chain reaction of war declarations that effectively ended the Concert of Europe, an era of relative peace between the Great Powers of Europe established upon the downfall of Napoleon 100 years prior. It has also been argued that nationalism sparked the conflict over the question of Serbian sovereignty in contested areas of the Western Balkans, notably in areas such as Bosnia that remained under the Austro-Hungarian Empire.[4] Many other studies of the war's roots look to economic and political disputes between the European powers, including issues over the control of commercial routes.[5] Countries such as Germany wanted to redistribute world economic power, something that could not be achieved without confronting both Britain and her allies, eventually including the United States.[6]

Yet another major catalyst of the war was the poorly conceived frontiers of many European countries.[7] These boundaries, set by centuries old multiethnic empires, cut across the fabric of European societies, dividing many national groups among states.

Since the Napoleonic Era, few great power conflicts had rocked Europe. Other than the Crimean and Franco-Prussian wars, most rivalries between European states took place as proxy wars throughout the European colonial realms. Great Britain had been the dominant power globally, but even prior to the war's outbreak there was talk of the coming "German Century" or "American Century" that would replace British hegemony.[8] The Great War was clearly a seminal moment in this shift. The mass mobilizations of 1914 ensured that World War I would not be another such limited war ending with minor border readjustments. The motives of the Great Powers differed, but it was German ambitions that were foremost. These included two main questions over war aims: 1) would Germany extend her preeminence beyond Central Europe, and 2) would Germany be able to force a change in colonial distributions globally?

American entry into the war in 1917 altered Germany's calculus dramatically. Initially, American entry effected greater economic impact than military, as it took a year to expand and mobilize the American forces for an overseas fight.[9] However, American entry proved decisive in turning the tide against Germany on the hitherto static Western Front—the great series of trenches running from the English Channel all the way to the Swiss border.

World War I marked the end of American isolationism and was only the first of many entanglements outside the Western Hemisphere entered into by the United States. Prior to World War I, America had been content to focus on its own internal expansion, but with the closing of the frontier, the United States was suddenly thrust onto the world stage. Border disputes among the European powers and internal European power politics played no part in the

American decision to intervene in the war. Instead, the United States had refrained from joining the conflict due both to isolationism and to a feeling that American economic interests would not be served by entry into the war. The United States finally declared war following the sinking of the American passenger ship *Lusitania* and the interception of the Zimmerman telegram, wherein the German imperial government offered Mexico an alliance and a return of formerly Mexican lands in the Southwestern United States if they entered on the side of the Central Powers.[10] This provocation led American President Woodrow Wilson, who just one year previously had campaigned for re-election under the slogan "He kept us out of the war," to call for a declaration of war on Germany and Austria-Hungary. It has also been argued that Wilson steered the United States into the war in order to gain a seat at the peace conference that would surely follow the conflict.[11] The United States never officially declared war on the other Central Powers—Ottoman Turkey and Bulgaria. The Americans also associated with the Allied side perceiving that Germany presented a greater economic threat to the United States than did Britain.[12] It is noteworthy that the United States never actually joined the Allies, but instead was an associated power outside the formal alliance structure.

President Wilson, in his initial message to Congress delivered when the declaration of war was made, remarked, "The world must be made safe for democracy."[13] With this remark, Wilson's ideals—the idea that the United States was not only joining the war for social and economic reasons, but to promote democracy and to forge a world of nation-states rather than empires and would end militarism, imperialism and war, and above all Bolshevism—became central to the United States war aims.[14] Wilson had three concepts that he believed would fix the problems that led to the war: 1) people needed the right to choose their sovereign affiliation (self-determination), 2) the world needed to show equal respect for the sovereign rights of strong and weak states, and 3) every people had the right to peaceful existence.[15] The decision by President Wilson to intervene marked a significant change in American foreign policy and paved the way for future American interventions around the world. American intervention also changed the very nature of the conflict. World War I became a war of liberation, rather than one of imperialist conquest. Just months after American entry, President Wilson presented the American war aims in his famous Fourteen Points address to Congress.

THE FOURTEEN POINTS†

I. Open covenants of peace, openly arrived at, after which there shall be no private international understandings of any kind but diplomacy shall proceed always frankly and in the public view.

II. Absolute freedom of navigation upon the seas, outside territorial waters, alike in peace and in war, except as the seas may be closed in whole or in part by international action for the enforcement of international covenants.

III. The removal, so far as possible, of all economic barriers and the establishment of an equality of trade conditions among all the nations consenting to the peace and associating themselves for its maintenance.

IV. Adequate guarantees given and taken that national armaments will be reduced to the lowest point consistent with domestic safety.

V. A free, open-minded, and absolutely impartial adjustment of all colonial claims, based upon a strict observance of the principle that in determining all such questions of sovereignty the interests of the populations concerned must have equal weight with the equitable claims of the government whose title is to be determined.

VI. The evacuation of all Russian territory and such a settlement of all questions affecting Russia as will secure the best and freest cooperation of the other nations of the world in obtaining for her an unhampered and unembarrassed opportunity for the independent determination of her own political development and national policy and assure her of a sincere welcome into the society of free nations under institutions of her own choosing; and, more than a welcome, assistance also of every kind that she may need and may herself desire. The treatment accorded Russia by her sister nations in the months to come will be the acid test of their good will, of their comprehension of her needs as distinguished from their own interests, and of their intelligent and unselfish sympathy.

VII. Belgium, the whole world will agree, must be evacuated and restored, without any attempt to limit the sovereignty which she enjoys in common with all other free nations. No other single act will serve as this will serve to restore confidence among the nations in the laws which they have themselves set and determined for the government of their relations with one another. Without this healing act the whole structure and validity of international law is forever impaired.

VIII. All French territory should be freed and the invaded portions restored, and the wrong done to France by Prussia in 1871 in the matter of Alsace-Lorraine, which has unsettled the peace of the world for nearly fifty years, should be righted, in order that peace may once more be made secure in the interest of all.

IX. A readjustment of the frontiers of Italy should be effected along clearly recognizable lines of nationality.

X. The peoples of Austria-Hungary, whose place among the nations we wish to see safeguarded and assured, should be accorded the freest opportunity to autonomous development.

XI. Rumania, Serbia, and Montenegro should be evacuated; occupied territories restored; Serbia accorded free and secure access to the sea; and the relations of the several Balkan states to one another determined by friendly counsel along historically established lines of allegiance and nationality; and international guarantees of the political and economic independence and territorial integrity of the several Balkan states should be entered into.

XII. The Turkish portion of the present Ottoman Empire should be assured a secure sovereignty, but the other nationalities which are now under Turkish rule should be assured an undoubted security of life and an absolutely unmolested opportunity of autonomous development, and the Dardanelles should be permanently opened as a free passage to the ships and commerce of all nations under international guarantees.

XIII. An independent Polish state should be erected which should include the territories inhabited by indisputably Polish populations, which should be assured a free and secure access to the sea, and whose political and economic independence and territorial integrity should be guaranteed by international covenant.

XIV. A general association of nations must be formed under specific covenants for the purpose of affording mutual guarantees of political independence and territorial integrity to great and small states alike.

† Address of President Wilson to Congress, January 8, 1918. In Arthur Link. *The Papers of Woodrow Wilson, Volume 45*. Princeton, Princeton University Press: 1984. Pg. 536.

Other countries would join the original Entente Powers (the United Kingdom, France and the Russian Empire) during the course of the war. Unlike the United States, states including Romania and Italy joined the Entente with the express promise that they would receive additional territory upon victory.[16] Much of this territory was promised in secret treaties between the powers, such as the Treaty of London—an agreement that would grant Italy large areas of the Austro-Hungarian Empire. The United States was not a party to these agreements and directly opposed them when declaring war, as made clear by the first of Wilson's Fourteen Points. The United States was only an associated power, rather than a direct ally, thus freeing it from any specific pledges to the Allied powers. By 1916, the Entente Powers envisioned a new Europe emerging after the war to replace the Austro-Hungarian Empire.[17] Not only the European map would change, as vast areas of the Middle East were under the control of the Central Powers, and the dispositions of these areas remained a key interest to the Allies. The settlements envisioned by the Allies would later prove difficult to reconcile with the ideals laid out by President Wilson's Fourteen Points. There was a clear division between the parties, as Europeans viewed American entry as protection from Germany, while Wilson viewed American entry primarily through the lens of a scholar, viewing America's role in a more detached manner than that of an Allied power.[18] These divisions would lead to several major crises at the forthcoming peace conference in 1919.

At 11:00 AM on November 11, 1918, World War I ended. The German Empire agreed to a cease-fire with the Allied countries, with the sole condition that the final peace settlement would follow the Fourteen Points laid out by President Wilson. At this time, British Prime Minister David Lloyd George famously remarked, "I hope we may say that thus, this fateful morning, came an end to all wars."[19] The horrors of trench warfare, suffering of refugees and civilians, and the use of poison gas all helped generate international consensus that another great war could not be allowed to happen. In the intervening years, much of the focus on the peace settlements has been on the League of Nations, the institution proposed as the last of Wilson's Fourteen Points, and on the economic problems associated with war reparations. Less attention has been paid to the borders redrawn at the end of the war, despite the fact that much of the American peace proposal focused on this very issue. In fact, eight of the Fourteen Points are expressly geographic, promising shifts in

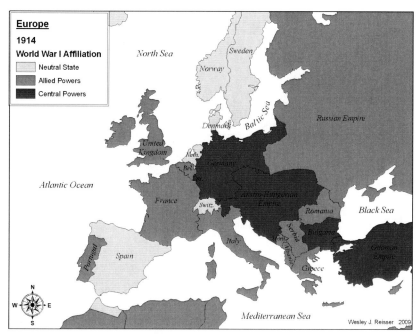

Figure 1.1. *Europe During World War I: As the war progressed, more states joined the Allies in opposition to the Central Powers. The original alliance of France, Britain, Russia, Serbia and Belgium expanded to include Italy, other Balkan states and eventually the United States. (Cartography by the author)*

territory in recognition of the self-determination of nations. President Wilson believed that people's interests could be best protected by living in their respective nation-states, thus leading to calls for territorial transfer and the creation of Poland in his Fourteen Points. Little did Wilson know that following the signing of the armistice with Germany, both Britain and France were ready to abandon his Fourteen Points. The Allies, not including the United States, worried about the centrality of the Fourteen Points to the armistice, especially as they had no internal accord on how to handle them and had never agreed to them.

In Paris, self-determination became the watchword of the day. Despite its centrality to the American mission, there is much debate over exactly what this meant. Wilson by no means created this concept, but it developed through profound changes in society, and Wilson both understood and could enunciate the concept better than other world leaders. Several key factors led to the need for this new mode of legitimacy; these included the increasing secularization of life in the late 19th century and

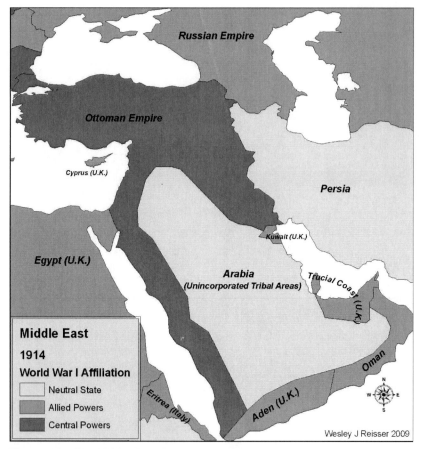

Figure 1.2. *The Middle East During World War I: The Ottoman Empire, although greatly diminished over the previous century, remained the dominant regional power. British colonies in the region gave the Allies a staging ground on this front of the conflict. (Cartography by the author)*

the downfall of traditional hierarchies, necessitating leaders to embrace new ways of justifying legitimacy.[20] Divine right no longer sufficed. Representing one's nation and claiming legitimacy through such a program came to replace earlier forms of political legitimacy. The Allied powers had been reluctant to embrace this Wilsonian program, but by 1917 both pressure from President Wilson and fear of the Bolsheviks led to their embrace of his program, at least nominally. Wilson viewed self-determination as the empowerment of individuals to vote for their leaders and express their political opinions, which he deemed deficient in Europe prior to the war.[21] How exactly this would be accomplished was less clear in the waning days of the conflict. British Prime Minister

David Lloyd George came around to embracing the concept, as he saw it as the only way to draw borders that would lead to a lasting peace.[22] The French chose to interpret self-determination differently, and saw it as the universal value of liberty, clearly separating political from ethno-cultural interpretations of self-determination.[23] This difference of interpretation would prove key in the end, leading to some of the most contentious debates at the peace conference. British diplomat and negotiator at the peace conference, Harold Nicolson, viewed the difference between the Anglo-American and French-Italian interpretations of self-determination as a "flagrant discrepancy."[24] These differing approaches to this key concept framed many of the most difficult debates seen at Paris.

The peace settlement signed in Paris the following year was anything but a carbon copy of Wilson's peace program. The Paris treaties changed the way that boundaries and territory were settled following conflict. The Inquiry, a commission established by the U.S. government, undertook immense amounts of research to understand better the demographic makeup of Europe, so that *scientifically* drawn boundaries would prevent the reemergence of border conflicts in that region. At the time, it was believed that a *scientific* peace was possible, an idea that has met increasing skepticism since. The Inquiry's work became one of the most significant cartographic projects in the 20th century, and ended by reshaping the map of Europe and the Middle East along with outlining principles for the future redrafting of borders around the world. The legacy of these treaties lives on today. As conflicts involving boundary issues continue, exploring how borders were redrawn in the past and how those borders have either calmed or exacerbated tensions helps shed light on whether re-demarcating boundaries remains an appropriate mechanism in furthering peace.

WILSONIAN PRINCIPLES

The set of ideas and ideals centering around self-determination and the creation of nation-states—collectively the Wilsonian Principles—established themselves as the defining characteristics of President Wilson's vision for the postwar world, and indeed have held up as basic principles in the international system. These ideas were revolutionary at the time of the Paris Peace Conference, thus leading to the controversies around them during peace negotiations.

The rise of these concepts in the late 19th century opened a new chapter in how we view political divisions throughout the world. On the eve of the First World War, most of the world was divided amongst multiethnic empires of many flavors. The British Empire, with only a small territorial base in Europe, controlled vast territories across the globe. The Ottoman Empire, although almost completely removed from Europe (except for the small Thracian area that remains in Turkey today) maintained Turkish dominance throughout the Middle East, with large regions inhabited by Arabs, Kurds and Armenians. Europe itself consisted primarily of large multiethnic states, with much of its territory split among the German, Austro-Hungarian and Russian Empires.

The promise of self-determination espoused by President Wilson made it necessary to group people into national units to properly account for their collective rights. Under his doctrine of self-determination, Wilson made it clear that every nation should have a say in the creation of its laws.[25] Rather than defining all subjects of a given state together, which proved especially problematic when considering large multiethnic empires, peoples were defined through their perceived membership in a national group.

At the time, scholars were attempting to define the nation in clearer terms than in earlier periods. Geographer Albert Perry Brigham defined nationality as a "unity of ideal, derived from hereditary experience and geographical environment."[26] He wrote that such groups wish to live and act together, as well as share a common government. He also noted that nations were not clearly defined racially. Many researchers from previous eras defined national identity partly on racial characteristics. This definition of nationality is inherently qualitative; due to this problem, use of such a definition would not be possible in scientifically determining what nation any given group of people belonged to, as there would be no data from which to draw upon.

Leon Dominian, a member of the Inquiry, wrote that nationality is an artificial product derived from race and shared history.[27] This concept has three fundamental elements: population, history and geography. Although today many nations may not use race in their definitions, the cohesive population that shares a common perceived history and geography continues to hold. However, even this definition fails to address concretely who fits into a specific nation in a measurable way.

Dominian, along with many other experts of the time, chose language as the best indicator of national identity. His book, *Frontiers of Language and Nationality in Europe*, uses language to define the different nations of Europe. Dominian states, "To separate the idea of language from nationality is rarely possible."[28] This marked a shift from earlier periods, as the cultural distinction of language became paramount over earlier foci on physical and military bounds between people.[29] Language was easily measurable through census data, and therefore offered a convenient means to define nationality.

However, language by itself did not a nation make. Dominian noted that geographical unity remained important in defining a nation.[30] For example, while English served as the primary language for several nations by the early 20th century, scholars would never have considered Americans, Englishmen or Australians to all be of one English nation by virtue of a common tongue. Scholars did not, however, extend a similar understanding to peoples living in Eastern Europe, as this was viewed as a geographically compact area. How this played out in a region like the Middle East, where most populations spoke Arabic dialects, but were often defined as part of differing nations, remained even less clear.

Wilson was well aware of some of the problems inherent in the concept of self-determination, particularly in places where multiple groups of people lived interspersed. Scholars preparing for the peace conference were aware that minority populations would continue to exist in the new Europe they were proposing. Therefore, there was agreement that small groups in each state should have the same freedom of language and religion as the majorities.[31] This was to be accomplished through the inclusion of minority treaties in the peace settlement. The Great Powers were very concerned with the minority treaty regime, enforced through the League of Nations, as it proved to threaten the integrity of some unwilling signatory states. Such treaties did not survive the interwar period.

The imperial state model prevailed prior to World War I, but following the war, the concept of the nation-state—that nations of people are best represented by their own state—dominated. Many scholars believed it was the best criterion for which state a people should live in.[32] However, this did not mean that every nation should have its own state, just that the peoples of a nation should be in the same state. At the outbreak of the war, Poles lived in three states (Germany, Austria-Hungary and Russia), Romanians in three as well (Romania, Austria-Hungary, and Russia)—so they stood out as examples of divided nations. Rectifying this problem became an important component of the American plan for peace in Europe.

Nationalism, as a concept, had risen to the fore in Europe in the previous century, leading to an ever-rising call for nation-states to replace the multiethnic empires of Europe.[33] The rise of nationalism led to a redefinition of empires, as lands once defined as multilingual or multireligious empires were suddenly recast as multiethnic or multinational.[34] The ensuing "Era of Romanticism" implied that defining nation through language, race and religion was at hand.[35] This idea essentially defined nation as a net shared culture that combined these characteristics. At first, political elites in the empires tried to enforce top-down nationalizing programs, but these backfired in many cases and led to bottom-up counter nationalisms.[36] These groups called for the redrawing of borders, thereby creating a new order that would supposedly impose a more just political framework, and hopefully one inherently more peaceful than that which preceded it. Western Europe needed only minor revisions to its territorial bounds, as the Western European nations had developed to fill in the borders of existing states. In some cases this transcended language, as in Alsace-Lorraine where German-speaking majorities were viewed by Wilson and the Inquiry to be French in nationality. In Eastern Europe, however, the lack of concurrence between cultural and political bounds led to the need for major territorial revision.[37]

For the first time, during this period, nationality was presented as the most legitimate basis for a state. This shift in defining the role of the state was one part of the larger leveling of spatial hierarchies in the pre–World War I era.[38] The doctrine of self-determination has become part and parcel with the concept of nationalism.[39] Nationalism scholar Hugh Seton-Watson points out:

> It was assumed in the age of President Wilson that states would embody nations; that the people of every state would form a nation; and that eventually, in the golden age of self-determination which was dawning, every nation would have a state.[40]

Previously, European dynasties had relied upon other factors to maintain their legitimacy and their failure to adapt led to their downfall. Stability, defense and divine right held the state together in earlier periods of European history. However, the rise of nationalism challenged the imperial order to its core. It is not surprising then that with the creation of the League of Nations and the closing of the age of dynasticism, the end of World War I marked the maturing of the nation-state concept as the new norm brought about the slow demise of the imperial order.[41]

THE INQUIRY—AMERICA'S SECRET PEACE PLANNING COMMISSION

A year prior to the end of the war, President Wilson convened a group of experts to begin laying out a proposal for peace. Wilson sought a *scientific* peace, meaning one in which the disinterested findings of specialists, rather than those of powered interests, would guide the outcome of the treaties.[42] This group of academics and leading foreign policy thinkers, under the leadership of Wilson's personal foreign policy advisor Colonel Edward M. House, gathered at the headquarters of the American Geographical Society (AGS) in New York City to begin proposals on what a final peace settlement should look like. Day-to-day operations came under the direction of House's close confidant, Sidney Mezes. To avoid arousing suspicion, this group assumed the name The Inquiry, as their mission remained a secret one. Geographer Neil Smith notes: "The Inquiry carries great significance in the history of U.S. foreign relations. For the first time, rather than simply responding to events, the government attempted to provide a systematic worldview ahead of time."[43] The Inquiry chose the AGS building both for its extensive holdings of geographical information and its distance from Washington, home to the prying eyes of Congress and the State Department. At the AGS building, the Inquiry had access to over 50,000 books and over 47,000 maps.[44] About 150 scholars convened in this project. The vast majority hailed from a small group of elite eastern universities, over half from just the AGS and four schools: Harvard, Yale, Columbia and Princeton.[45] It is likely that Wilson's background as a university president led him to trust scholars rather than bureaucrats with this challenge. Wilson's creation of the Inquiry was an explicitly geopolitical mandate, one to collect data, compare claims and map possible boundaries.[46] Economic matters were also handled by the Inquiry, although they make up a much smaller portion of the total reports.[47] Great Britain and France each created similar organizations, reaching drastically different conclusions from those of the American experts. These groups had very little contact prior to the peace conference.

Although many personalities stand out as a major figures within the Inquiry, none stand out more so than Isaiah Bowman, then Director of the AGS. Bowman's role achieved international importance due to his influence in the shaping of the final treaties. Bowman served as Chief Territorial Specialist, but attained day-to-day control of the Inquiry from Mezes within months of the organization's founding. Bowman donated use of the AGS building to the Inquiry, applying this as leverage toward wresting control of the organization, along with the significant geographic competence that he brought to the mission.[48]

Bowman was a seminal figure in the history of modern geography. He envisioned political geography as a tool to identify problems such as protection of minorities or national boundaries. Rather than questioning the state itself, as did many later scholars, he paid attention to pressing problems of the time and utilized geographical information to help solve them. This outlook manifested in the solutions Bowman presented in the Inquiry reports. In dealing with problems of territory, Bowman would prove to be one of Wilson's closest confidantes and a central figure at the Paris Peace Conference. Bowman represented the United States on several commissions in Paris, most notably on the Polish Commission. He would later serve as a territorial expert again for President Roosevelt during World War II. Writing in the aftermath of that war, Bowman reflected on the nature of territorial decisions more broadly, after twice confronting them on the international scene:

> Territorial decisions involve all the complexities of civilization—historical fitness, population mobility, resource distributions, tax bases, divisions of agricultural fertility zones, and a thousand other considerations. Territory is not an abstraction. Unfortunately, nations can not be separated approximately. A boundary has to be here, not hereabouts.[49]

Bowman, along with his Inquiry colleagues faced a daunting task in preparing a peace plan for the American delegation.

The Inquiry presented its initial suggestions on American strengths and negotiating positions in a memorandum to the President on December 22, 1917.[50] A published report followed on January 21, 1919, for the principal officials sent to Paris, including President Wilson, entitled "Outline of Tentative Report and Recommendations Prepared by the Intelligence Section, in Accordance with Instructions, for the President and Plenipotentiaries." This became better known as the "Black Book," and contained specific negotiating points and proposed border revisions for parts of Europe and the Middle East. A much shorter "Red Book" followed soon thereafter, which covered colonial problems, mostly those involving German colonies in Africa and the Pacific.

The Inquiry believed that through the acquisition of data on each state it would be able to provide unbiased advice for the American delegation. Most of the Inquiry's recommendations focused on issues of territory, thus offering geographers a major role in the process. Bowman, as the lead territorial specialist, and his staff faced an enormous task in gathering the vast data necessary to provide recommendations to the negotiators. The U.S. tradition of isolationism left the Inquiry with no immediate experience of European internal politics and trends, giving them less direction than their European counterparts. On the upside, isolationism left the United States with a disinterested outlook.[51] This distanced view aided in the perception that American reports were less biased than those of other states' intelligence organizations. The Inquiry identified a plethora of territorial issues that would arise at the peace conference and therefore require an American position. Among them were:

1. Territories whose status was fixed by prior agreements (ex. Belgium, Northern France)
2. Territories under military control where self-determination was to be applied (ex. Germany's eastern frontier)
3. New states seeking admission to the family of nations (ex. Finland, Ukraine and the Arab states)
4. States within which oppressed nationalities required protection (ex. Turkey and in the Balkans)
5. States less than fully sovereign seeking a more independent status (ex. Persia, Afghanistan and China)
6. States under belligerent occupation where no national consciousness exists (ex. African and Pacific island colonies)
7. Spheres of influence established before and during the war (ex. Far East and Africa)
8. Territories formally annexed during the war (ex. Parts of Romania)
9. Territory claimed by belligerents to complete their national unity
10. Territory claimed by belligerents for strategic value

11. Territory claimed by belligerents for economic value
12. Territory claimed by belligerents on historical grounds
13. Rights of way and other privileges claimed by one state in the territory of another (ex. Poland's and Serbia's access to the sea)
14. Exchanges of territory
15. The control of international rivers
16. The control of narrow seas
17. The extension of territorial waters[52]

Many of the territorial problems encountered by the Inquiry combined multiple aspects, thus creating the need for complex analysis of the problems that the conference would have to resolve. In this time period, it was not uncommon to rank groups of people in hierarchies based upon ability to govern themselves, thus leading to recommendations that some areas gain self-government while others be made into mandates (supervised colonies). Eventually, the key territorial issues identified were collated into the Black Book and Red Book.

In the end, the Inquiry's 150 scholars produced nearly 2,000 reports and 1,200 maps.[53] Despite this prolific output, the geographers of the Inquiry faced a severe handicap, in that political geography was but a newly emerging field. They faced further problems stemming from the ambiguity of the Fourteen Points, the founding principles which their recommendations needed to match. Other than Poland, the Fourteen Points do not explicitly call for the creation of any new states, and they only suggest some border realignments, such as those in Alsace-Lorraine and along the Austro-Italian border. The facts on the ground shifted dramatically in the closing days of the war, resulting in final recommendations that often contradicted Wilson's earlier stated intentions.

The Inquiry not only focused on geography, but also principally on problems in Europe and adjacent areas in the Middle East. Although the Inquiry produced many studies on issues in the Middle East, Africa and even Latin America, 51 percent of the reports issued by the Inquiry focused on Europe.[54] The Inquiry produced 263 major reports on Europe during its work prior to the conference. This included 47 reports on Germany (Germany accounted for17 percent of the total reports), 52 on Austria-Hungary (20 percent), and 63 on the Balkans (24 percent). This focus on Central and Eastern Europe indicates the controversiality of the outstanding problems in these areas. The largest geographical issues at the conference were at stake in these regions. These reports also focused on the locations of postwar boundaries with the assumption that not only boundaries would shift, but also that new countries would be formed. The other region most examined in the Inquiry reports is the lands of the Ottoman Empire, especially analyzing the regions of the Kurds and modern Iraq, as well as the creation of a Jewish state in Palestine. Just as European boundary problems would continue to plague the world long after the peace conference, many of those in the Middle East remain unresolved to this very day.

In the peace settlement, the Inquiry employed the recently formulated concept of national self-determination as the primary factor in determining how borders should be rearranged. Geographical historian Geoffrey Martin notes, "The Paris variety of Wilsonian idealism was born with the Inquiry: democracy, self determination, accommodation, justice became guidelines to Inquiry endeavors."[55] As used by Wilson, self-determination meant the right of each national group to determine their own political destiny, usually through the creation of an independent state. Self-determination became the watchword of the day, but the competing nationalisms of the regions concerned made this a difficult concept from which to build peace.[56] This would prove the case because in many areas there was, and indeed today still are, a great number of peoples living in one region. In some regions, it would turn out to be impossible to use self-determination in electing an appropriate boundary.[57] Inquiry geographers, such as Leon Dominian, came to believe that Western Europe had consolidated into political units based on language, whereas Eastern Europe remained a tangle of groups.[58] Dominian recommended that linguistic lines be used to make the border adjustments between states in Eastern Europe, which became the primary method enlisted in the Inquiry reports. Others favored the use of a plebiscite to allow affected peoples a say in their own self-determination. Although plebiscites were called for by the Inquiry in several areas, most border recommendations given by the Black Book and other reports did not.

Some experts, such as Inquiry economist Simon Patten, recommended the new Europe not follow lines of self-determination at all. They believed this was an untenable proposition, positing the overlap of linguistic groups would lead to "perpetual disputes" among them.[59] These dissenters called for a new arrangement in Europe with economically based boundaries that would create cohesive and efficient economic zones on the continent. Their arguments went mostly unheeded at the time.

Those in favor of a peace based on national self-determination emerged victorious in the Inquiry reports. Although language was the primary method relied upon, other factors such as religion, demography, occupation and the urban/rural split also were used by Inquiry geographers in determining what nationality an area was currently populated by. The Inquiry geographers faced an especially difficult problem in determining which nationalisms were "well-defined" enough to warrant a state.[60] It was widely agreed that some nations were not developed enough politically to form their own states; however, no definition emerged to determine what was well-defined, leading to endless possibilities on what frontiers should be proposed.

Along with its scores of reports, the Inquiry geographers produced many maps that proved important tools for the American delegation and for the Paris Peace Conference as a whole. Many of the maps produced for the President provided not just the old border lines, but also the borders promised in secret treaties and tentative suggestions by the Inquiry staff as to where new borders should be drawn.[61] In their reports, the Inquiry emphasized their maps were objective and scientific while those produced by other delegations were biased and partisan.[62] Professional geographers drew the borders in the former case, and statesmen without the requisite theoretical background in the latter. In truth, the Inquiry staff remained susceptible to political leanings and therefore included significant bias in their maps.

Even so, the impact of the Inquiry maps can be seen in that Isaiah Bowman's base map of Europe was the most cited map at the Paris Peace Conference, serving as a basis for negotiations throughout the European region.[63] The plans proposed by the Inquiry were adopted in many circumstances, thus making the Inquiry a major force in the shaping of political boundaries in the postwar world.

THE PARIS PEACE CONFERENCE

In January 1919, President Wilson boarded the USS *George Washington* and headed to Paris for the peace conference. Great hopes were pinned to his upcoming involvement in negotiations. The famous economist John Maynard Keynes, a member of the British delegation, noted Wilson's standing at the time:

> When President Wilson left Washington he enjoyed a prestige and a moral influence throughout the world unequaled in history. His bold and measured words carried the peoples of Europe above and beyond the voices of their own politicians. The enemy peoples trusted him to carry out the compact he had made with them; and the Allied people acknowledged him not as a victor but almost a prophet.[64]

The 1919 Paris Peace Conference was a unique event, bringing together more groups to negotiate a settlement than the world had ever witnessed before.[65] Representatives of not just the Great Powers, but also small states, nations without states, states that were not even involved in the war, and many special interest groups traveled to Paris to provide input into the settlement and the creation of the League of Nations. Paris was practically overrun by parties looking for a role in the settlement: "During the winter and spring of 1918–1919 Paris was the Mecca for the oppressed not alone of Europe but of the earth."[66] Many expected Wilson's Fourteen Points to be the foundation for the settlement; however, major European powers, particularly France, expected modifications on issues including territorial settlements and reparations. The United Kingdom came to the table with more in common with the American position, but was adamantly opposed to freedom of the seas as part of a final settlement. This placed the American plan in direct opposition to those wishing to impose an imperial peace. Overall, there remained an expectation that the new settlement would be very different from that of previous European wars. Whereas in the past, victors helped themselves to whatever they wanted from the defeated power, a new order was expected to emerge from the conference that would equitably divide assets and allow the emergence of a new peaceful world order. Many issues would be covered including reparations, the League of Nations, economic settlements and international labor arrangements, but it was first and foremost about territory.

The Americans remained in a unique position as the only belligerent viewed as neutral toward the final settlement's terms. America had no territorial claims being contested in the conference and also did not expect war reparations from the Central Powers. Wilson had been clear from the outset of American involvement that the United States did not enter the war for selfish reasons such as territory, tribute or revenge.[67] This provided the delegation with significant influence at the negotiating table, despite America's relative low number of casualties as compared to other major involved powers, especially France, the United Kingdom and Italy. (Bolshevik Russia was not included, as they had concluded a separate peace with Germany in 1918 with the Treaty of Brest-Litovsk.)

The United States brought other assets and liabilities to Paris. The assets included: the enormous economic power that America possessed relative to the other powers at the time of the armistice, a better relationship with Austria-Hungary than the other parties, and intangibles such as the almost universal feeling that old style diplomacy was bankrupt and the hope that much of the world had placed in Wilson's proposal for the League of Nations.[68] The United States also faced additional liabilities, including the American public's unwillingness for another military offensive that could result in a war of attrition and a possible invasion of the Middle East. This lack of a military option if the conference failed blunted the otherwise strong American military position.

President Wilson traveled with a huge delegation across the Atlantic, bringing many members of the Inquiry. Beneath the American plenipotentiaries (President Wilson, Secretary of State Robert Lansing, Colonel House and General Tasker Bliss) existed a large organization. This included a Secretariat to handle the delegation's day-to-day needs, a group of technical advisors for military and legal issues, and the Bureau of Inquiry Territorial and Trade Adjustments.[69] Colonel House and Dr. Sidney Mezes headed the Inquiry Bureau, and Isaiah Bowman led the territorial division, with this division accounting for the largest portion of the American delegation, including experts not just on Europe, but on every other part of the globe as well. On his way to the conference, President Wilson spoke with members of the Inquiry where he promised, "You tell me what's right and I'll fight for it."[70] He judged the mood of the Allied leaders as "brutal, greedy and intransigent."[71] Prior to the conference, Wilson committed himself to facts in formulating the final peace, rather than allowing the power politics of old to hold sway over the final peace treaties. Once in Paris, American scholars were tasked to talk with leaders of the nascent nations, thus thrusting them into the role of diplomats, rather than just advisors.[72] By the conference's opening, the Inquiry was firmly entrenched as a highly influential advisory body to the American plenipotentiaries.

The unique role played by scholars at the Paris Peace Conference was already well understood by the time the conference began. A memorandum circulated in the early days of the conference by the American delegation lays this out:

> The Intelligence Section of the American Commission to Negotiate Peace, dealing with the territorial, economic, and political matters which come before the peace conference, represents a new idea in international relations—the idea of utilizing the expert services of scholars in determining the facts that should be the bases of the peace settlements. The Intelligence Section is an outgrowth of the Inquiry, a group of men engaged during more than a year past in gathering material for the peace conference under the direction of Colonel House. Similar organizations have been at work in France and England....
>
> Actual experience at the peace conference has shown the soundness of these anticipations, since in almost every case the discussion of a question has involved the appointment of special committees who are to hear the facts and report to the Bureau. It is surprising to what an extent the impartial discussion of disputed points has led to unanimity of opinion, even on the part of nations directly interested in a given solution. The whole process marks a new stage in the development of better international relations, since it carries over into a field of international relations the good will which has always existed in the world between scholars expert in the same subject. It may be doubted whether at any time in the future complicated problems of world politics will be discussed without reference to expert bodies like those now working out the intricacies of European politics, ethnography, resources, waterways, ports, railroads, canals, topography, etc.
>
> The experiment has been attended by some very interesting results. In the case of the American experts an appeal was made to the colleges and universities and private and public institutions of various kinds in the United States for the loan of men and material, and to all such requests the most hearty response was obtained. It became a kind of joint educational enterprise which elicited the enthusiasm and devotion of a large group of strong men at a time of need when everyone was seeking to be of the largest service to the national government.
>
> The work of the American experts was carried on at the building of the American Geographical Society... where there was made available the largest collection of carefully selected maps in the United States and the best geographical library as well.[73]

Once the conference opened, several groups were created to handle the negotiations and shape the new treaties. A large conference group consisting of every represented nation was set up along with a Council of Ten and a Council of Five, later the Council of Four (once Japan was no longer invited to the meetings). The Central Powers were not represented in any of these bodies or allowed a part in the negotiated settlement. Rather, they would be presented with final terms and then allowed to suggest revisions, although these were never considered. The real decisions were made in the Council of Four (the United States, France, the United Kingdom and Italy), also known by the moniker of the "Big Four." Of these Wilson was the only one not on the defensive, due to his efforts to create a new liberal international order.[74] The other sessions of the conference mainly served as ritual occasions. Small states and interested parties often addressed the Big Four, one at a time, and only on issues directly related to them. The creation of the Council of Four marked a turn where decisions could be made without the bother of territorial experts and with only political facts being considered.[75]

The dynamic that developed among the Big Four thus played the primary role in determining the outcomes of the conference. At the outset, Wilson perceived France as his best ally in the Big Four in the person of Prime Minister Georges Clemenceau. In the days leading up to the conference, Clemenceau remarked that only America and France desired an unselfish settlement, and he wanted to be involved with Wilson in upholding a new, more ethical era for the world.[76] This was not to last. As the conference wore on, Prime Minister Clemenceau made clear his disregard for the Fourteen Points.[77] In the end, the Americans viewed France more as an intransigent party than a helpful one in the negotiations.[78]

The second major player, the United Kingdom, became America's closest negotiating partner among the Big Four as the conference continued. Prime Minister David Lloyd George led the British delegation. Although the British and American interests on freedom of the seas differed, the British nurtured no territorial claims in Europe, thus allying them more closely to the American camp. The British delegation also aligned closely with the Americans by setting up direct cooperation between the American and British experts on territorial issues.[79] This included regular meetings between Inquiry members and their counterparts in the British delegation, such as Harold Nicolson.

The final member of the Big Four proved the most difficult for the other parties to work with. This was the Italian delegation led by Prime Minister Vittorio Orlando. Just as the United States, Italy entered the war late. However, Italy joined the Entente Powers following the secret

Treaty of London, in which Britain and France promised Italy large territorial concessions along the Austro-Hungarian frontier, in Albania, and in Turkey. President Wilson denied knowledge of these treaties and refused to recognize their validity at the conference. This eventually led to an Italian walkout from the conference at the height of negotiations. Italy would soon return, but the breech poisoned the relationship between Orlando and Wilson for the remainder of the conference.

In the end, the Big Four had to make major compromises to prevent the decomposition of Europe into ever smaller subdivisions based on nationality, and to draw borders that were as rational as possible. They presented the infamous Treaty of Versailles to Germany as the first major treaty at the conference. Other similar treaties, including the Austrian Treaty of St. Germain and the Hungarian Treaty of Trianon, were based on the Versailles treaty, but not completed until after Wilson and Lloyd George left Paris.[80] These treaties greatly altered the map of Europe. It would take another three years to finalize the settlement with

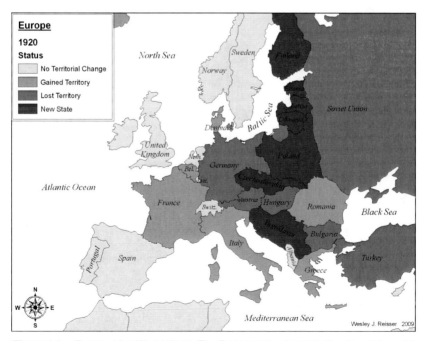

Figure 1.3. *Europe After World War I: The Paris treaties dramatically altered the political map of Europe. Many new countries emerged, while Allied states gained territory at the expense of the Central Powers and Russia, which had made a separate peace with Germany following the Bolshevik Revolution. (Cartography by the author)*

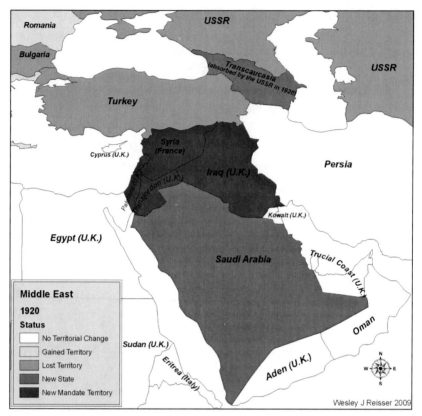

Figure 1.4.   *The Middle East After World War I: The dismantling of the Ottoman Empire led to the creation of French and British mandates, along with the recognition of the new Arab state of Saudi Arabia. (Cartography by the author)*

Turkey, due to the strife associated with Mustafa Kemal's revolution that created the Turkish nation-state out of the ashes of the Ottoman Empire. Just as with the European settlements, the Middle Eastern ones resulted in dramatic changes in boundaries.

Another set of treaties placed under the auspices of the League of Nations were created for many of the countries of Central and Eastern Europe to regulate the treatment of minorities in these areas. The mistreatment of minorities had concerned many in the Inquiry, and they were aware that only through ending this repression was there any chance of full reconciliation and peace in Europe.[81] In the end, fourteen countries with a combined population of 110 million were forced to sign minority treaties, which laid out specific rights and representation for minority groups within those states.[82] Due to the inability to separate all national groups by borders, this was viewed as the best method to protect those groups not in the majority in the state in which they were placed.

The Paris Peace Conference applied the concept of national self-determination more fully than ever before.[83] However, the settlement remained flawed in many ways. Germany had expected mild terms in the final settlement, expecting only to lose Alsace-Lorraine and a small amount of eastern territory, along with no reparations. However, the Germans viewed the final settlement as unduly harsh, with Hitler later referring to the treaty as a "diktat"—fully dictated with no German input. The French, on the other hand, felt that Germany got off too easy. Wilson managed to reduce the demands of the French delegation. More than any other issue, the territorial settlements are central to understanding and judging the treaties of World War I.[84] A host of domestic pressures and conflicting claims eventually overwhelmed the peacemakers, leading to the deals and compromises of Paris that have reverberated throughout the 20th century. Although many view the treaties in a negative light, Wilson's idealism and generosity toward a defeated opponent have inspired many, and Wilson perhaps laid the foundation for a better world than the one he was viewing in the immediate aftermath of the war.

WHAT HAPPENED TO THE AMERICAN PLAN FOR PEACE?

The World War I peace settlements resulted in many border changes throughout the world. In the years following, these have come under scrutiny. Edward House, close confidant of Woodrow Wilson and one the American plenipotentiaries, noted after the war:

> In the matter of boundaries the Paris Peace Conference was confronted with its most difficult problem. There was no good way out, and any decision was certain to displease, and in many instances do injustice.[85]

The Paris settlements increased European borders by more than two thousand miles.[86] Many of the most drastic changes occurred in Eastern Europe and the Middle East. The Austro-Hungarian Empire's problems were noted as especially acute in discussions at the conference, and it was in the areas of the Hapsburg, Romanov and Ottoman Empires where the most dramatic cartographic changes emerged postwar.

Since all historic events are set in space, understanding the geographic component is intrinsic to the character and meaning of these settlements and their effects. This is especially the case when analyzing events like the Paris Peace Conference. One American attendee, Charles Seymour, noted: "Every historical peace negotiation is inevitably based upon geography, since land and material wealth has been a fundamental objective of warring nations."[87] Despite this, most analysis of the treaties has focused on other issues while treating the territorial component of the treaties as only secondary in their ongoing impacts.

Although many legacies can be tied to the Paris treaties, a few truly stand out. The lasting impact of the call for national self-determination continues to this day. It is rare that a group calling for independence uses language other than that couched in terms compatible with those espoused by Woodrow Wilson. Indeed, Wilsonian ideals continue to reverberate throughout the diplomatic discourse of the 20th century. Even more importantly, the language of the state has shifted so much that today we live in a world of so-called nation-states, while the world that existed prior to the war was truly a world of empires. This is more than a semantic shift, as the new world order envisioned by Wilson has totally changed the role states play in the international system and how they justify their existence to each other.

Geography has not fully played its part in presenting a strong analysis of the peace settlements of World War I. This remains an important task, as ethnic and national conflicts continue in areas where the borders changed from this peace. The world still lives with many of the borders set at Paris and with the consequences of these decisions. Despite this, the overall scholarly focus on World War I has centered on two non-geographic factors: the issue of German reparations and the failure of the League of Nations (mainly due to the U.S. Senate's rejection of the Treaty of Versailles).

The re-drawing of the world map stands as another lasting legacy of the Paris Peace Conference. Many international borders drawn at the conference remain to this very day, including a vast number of borders proposed by the Inquiry and the American delegation. Border drawing involved the widespread use of geographic information by the Big Four, including a large number of maps. Many descriptions of policymakers huddling on the floor poring over maps survive from the conference. As this was the first time that principles beyond "to the victor go the spoils" were used, a thorough study of the use of maps and the legacy of the decisions made from such information provides key insights into the roles geographic information can play in peace processes. The following sums up this question: How did the American plan for peace, and especially its maps, influence the World War I peace treaties' final outcomes and what process did these proposals follow from initial proposal to final settlement? The following story will illuminate how maps were used by peacemakers, how new maps were drawn and how this process led to the remaking of the world map. Although the principal focus will remain the World War I peace treaties, I hope to illustrate these processes in a way that aids in the understanding of the border making process more generally, as well as investigating the power of maps in influencing policy makers. Although no war since has led to such large changes in international boundaries through a single peace settlement (the World War II border changes took place through a series of agreements and settlements, none involving all of the Allied powers), the world map continues to change to this day—most recently with the division of Sudan into two states in the summer of 2011. Border drawing remains an important component of peacemaking processes, as can be seen in the importance placed on border drawing in cases like the Israel-Palestinian conflict and the breakup of Yugoslavia. As the World War I treaties were the first to attempt to draw borders based on nationality, they provide the key to understanding these more recent border changes. Finally, an analysis of the Wilsonian program related to borders better illuminates his role at the Paris Peace Conference. Many criticisms of Wilson center on the final treaties not living up to the principles which he enunciated. These critiques fail to address the initial proposals Wilson brought to the table, many of which were scuttled by the other members of the Big Four, and, as will be seen, aligned closely with the principles he so eloquently enunciated prior to the end of the First World War.

NOTES

1. David Stevenson. 2004. *Cataclysm: The First World War as Political Tragedy.* New York: Basic Books.
2. Stephen Kern. 1983. *The Culture of Time and Space: 1880–1918.* Cambridge, MA: Harvard University Press.

3. John O'Loughlin and Herman van der Wusten. 1993. "Political Geography of War and Peace," in *Political Geography of the Twentieth Century* ed. P.J. Taylor. New York: John Wiley & Sons.

4. Stuart Woolf. 1996. *Nationalism in Europe, 1815 to the Present: A Reader*. London: Routledge.

5. Brian Blouet. 2001. *Geopolitics and Globalization in the Twentieth Century*. London: Reaktion Books. Simon Patten. 1915. "Unnatural Boundaries of European States." *Survey* (34).

6. John Agnew. 1998. *Geopolitics: Re-Visioning World Politics*. New York: Routledge.

7. Leon Dominian. 1917. *Frontiers of Language and Nationality in Europe*. New York: Henry Holt and Company.

8. P.J. Taylor. 1993. *Political Geography of the Twentieth Century*. New York: John Wiley & Sons.

9. Paul Kennedy. 1987. *The Rise and Fall of the Great Powers*. New York: Random House.

10. Stevenson 2004.

11. Niall Ferguson. 2006. *The War of the World: Twentieth Century Conflict and the Descent of the West*. New York: Penguin.

12. John Agnew. 1993. "The United States and American Hegemony," in *Political Geography of the Twentieth Century*, ed. P.J. Taylor. New York: John Wiley & Sons.

13. Address of President Wilson to Congress on April 2, 1917. In *President Wilson's Great Speeches*. Chicago: Stanton & Van Vliet. Pg. 20.

14. Amos Perlmutter. 1997. *Making the World Safe for Democracy: A Century of Wilsonianism and Its Totalitarian Challengers*. Chapel Hill: University of North Carolina Press.

15. Lawrence Gelfand. 1963. *The Inquiry: American Preparations for Peace 1917–1919*. New Haven: Yale University Press.

16. Blouet 2001.

17. Solomon Wank. 1997. "The Hapsburg Empire," in Karen Barkey and Mark von Hagen, *After Empire: Multiethnic Societies and Nation-Building*. Boulder, CO: Westview Press.

18. Frank Simonds. 1927. *How Europe Made Peace without America*. Garden City: Doubleday, Page and Co.

19. Parliamentary Debate of November 11, 1918. In *Hansard Parliamentary Debates (Commons) 5th Series*. London: Government of the United Kingdom. Pg. 2452.

20. Kern 1983, Pg. 178.

21. George White. 2004. *Nation, State, and Territory: Origins, Evolutions, and Relationships, Volume 1*. Lanham, MD: Rowman & Littlefield.

22. George Goldberg. 1969. *The Peace to End Peace: The Paris Peace Conference of 1919.* New York: Harcourt, Brace & World, Inc.

23. Rogers Brubaker. 1992. *Citizenship and Nationhood in France and Germany.* Cambridge, MA: Harvard University Press.

24. Harold Nicolson. 1933. *Peacemaking 1919.* London: Constable & Co. Pg. xv.

25. David Knight. 1982. "Identity and Territory: Geographical Perspectives on Nationalism and Regionalism." *Annals of the Association of American Geographers* (72:4).

26. Albert Perry Brigham. 1919. "Principles in the Determination of Boundaries." *Geographical Review* (7:4).

27. Dominian 1917.

28. Dominian 1917. Pg. 1.

29. Julian Minghi. 1963 (ii). "Boundary Studies in Political Geography." *Annals of the Association of American Geographers* (53:3).

30. Dominian 1917.

31. Patten 1915.

32. Brigham 1919.

33. Agnew 1998.

34. Hugh Seton-Watson. 1977. *Nations and States: An Enquiry into the Origins of Nations and the Politics of Nationalism.* Boulder, CO: Westview Press.

35. George White. 2000. *Nationalism and Territory: Constructing Group Identity in Southeastern Europe.* Lanham, MD: Rowman & Littlefield Publishers.

36. Charles Tilly. 1996. "The State of Nationalism." *Critical Review* (10:2).

37. Knight 1982.

38. Kern 1983.

39. Ibid.

40. Seton-Watson 1977, Pg. 1.

41. Ibid.

42. Gelfand 1963.

43. Neil Smith. 2003. *American Empire: Roosevelt's Geographer and the Prelude to Globalization.* Berkeley: University of California Press. Pg. 135.

44. Geoffrey Martin. 1968. *Mark Jefferson: Geographer.* Ypsilanti, MI: Eastern Michigan University Press.

45. Gelfand 1963.

46. Jeremy Crampton. 2006. "The Cartographic Calculation of Space: Race Mapping and the Balkans at the Paris Peace Conferece of 1919." *Social and Cultural Geography* (7:5).

47. Sidney Mezes. 1921. "Preparations for Peace," in *What Really Happened at Paris: The Story of the Peace Conference, 1918–1919 by American Delegates*, ed. Edward House. New York: Charles Scribner's Sons.

48. Gelfand 1963.

49. Isaiah Bowman. 1946. "The Strategy of Territorial Decisions." *Foreign Affairs* (24:2). Pg. 180.

50. Inquiry Document #887, "The Present Situation: The War Aims and Peace Terms It Suggests," 12/22/1917: U.S. Department of State. *Foreign Relations of the United States* (FRUS) Vol. 1, Pgs. 41–53.

51. Martin 1968.

52. Inquiry Document #890, "Mr. Walter Lippmann to Dr. S.E. Mezes and Mr. D.H. Miller," 4/17/1918: FRUS Vol. I, Pgs. 72–74.

53. Gelfand 1963, Pg. x.

54. Gelfand 1963.

55. Martin 1968, Pg. 169.

56. Margaret MacMillan. 2001. *Paris 1919*. New York: Random House.

57. Wesley Reisser. 2009. "Self-Determination and the Difficulty of Creating Nation-States—The Transylvania Case." *Geographical Review* (99:2).

58. Leon Dominian. 1918. "The Nationality Map of Europe," in *League of Nations*. Boston: World Peace Foundation.

59. Patten 1915.

60. MacMillan 2001.

61. Geoffrey Martin. 1980. *The Life and Thought of Isaiah Bowman*. Hamden, CT: Archon Books.

62. Jeremy Crampton. 2003. "Can We Learn from the Paris Peace Conference of 1919?" *Geoworld*.

63. Isaiah Bowman. *undated*. "The Geographical Program of the American Peace Delegation, 1919." Johns Hopkins University (JHU) Bowman Papers, MS 58 Box 13.3. Martin 1980.

64. John M. Keynes. 1920. *The Economic Consequences of the Peace*. New York: Harcourt, Brace and Howe. Pg. 38.

65. MacMillan 2001.

66. Edward House. 1921. "The Versailles Peace in Retrospect," in *What Really Happened at Paris: The Story of the Peace Conference, 1918–1919 by American Delegates*, ed. Edward House. New York: Charles Scribner's Sons. Pg. 431.

67. MacMillan 2001.

68. Inquiry Document #887, "The Present Situation: The War Aims and Peace Terms It Suggests," 12/22/1917: FRUS Vol. 1, Pgs. 41–53.

69. Dr. S.E. Mezes to the Secretary of State, 10/25/1918: FRUS Vol. I, Pgs. 111–112.

70. MacMillan 2001, Pg. 8.

71. Bullitt Lowry. 1996. *Armistice 1918*. Kent, OH: Kent State Press. Pg. 172.

72. Arthur Walworth. 1986. *Wilson and His Peacemakers: American Diplomacy at the Paris Peace Conference, 1919*. New York: W.W. Norton and Company.

73. Memorandum Regarding the Section of Territorial, Economic and Political Intelligence of the Commission to Negotiate Peace, undated: FRUS Vol. I, Pg. 183.

74. Perlmutter 1997.

75. Isaiah Bowman. 1921. "Constantinople and the Balkans," in *What Really Happened at Paris: The Story of the Peace Conference, 1918–1919 by American Delegates*, ed. Edward House. New York: Charles Scribner's Sons.

76. The Special Representative (House) to President Wilson: FRUS Vol. I, Pg. 344.

77. Keynes 1920.

78. MacMillan 2001.

79. Mr. D.H. Miller to Colonel E.M. House: FRUS Vol. I, Pgs. 338–339.

80. Stevenson 2004.

81. Patten 1915.

82. Isaiah Bowman. 1928. *The New World: Problems in Political Geography*. New York: World Book.

83. Norman Hill. 1945. *Claims to Territory in International Law and Relations*. London: Oxford University. Robert Lord. 1921. "Poland," in *What Really Happened at Paris: The Story of the Peace Conference, 1918–1919 by American Delegates*, ed. Edward House. New York: Charles Scribner's Sons.

84. Winston Churchill. 1960. "The World Crisis: The Territorial Settlements of 1919–1920," in Ido Lederer, *The Versailles Settlement: Was It Foredoomed to Failure?* Boston: DC Heath & Co.

85. House 1921, Pg. 429.

86. Bowman 1928.

87. Charles Seymour. 1960. "Geography, Justice, and Politics at the Paris Peace Conference of 1919," in *The Versailles Settlement: Was It Foredoomed to Failure?* ed. Ivo Lederer. Boston: DC Heath & Co. Pg. 106.

CHAPTER 2

"The Black Book"—A Blueprint for Peace

Prior to the start of the Paris Peace Conference, the American Inquiry prepared a single document, the so-called Black Book, that would serve as the principal policy document for the American delegation during the upcoming negotiations. Rather than using countless detailed Inquiry reports to inform on decisions, a single concise document was needed for background and a starting position for negotiators. This Black Book, officially titled "Outline of Tentative Report and Recommendations Prepared by the Intelligence Section, in Accordance with Instructions, for the President and Plenipotentiaries," was presented to President Wilson on January 21, 1919.[1] In 98 pages, the Inquiry summed up the recommended negotiating positions for the United States on a variety of issues, devoting 79 pages to territorial issues, 6 pages to economic issues and 5 pages to labor issues.[2] This entire report fit neatly into a black binder, thereby making it easy to take to negotiations, unlike longer reports or large format maps, which were used less often. The Black Book contained more than just text, but also a large collection of maps, some 23 in the final version, each just one regular-sized sheet of paper. This book would go on to greatly influence the final policy decisions made in Paris, and indeed redraw the map of the world.

Many scholars have mentioned the Black Book in their work on the Paris Peace Conference. One of its earliest mentions comes from Simon Mezes, Executive Director of the Inquiry, who wrote that the Black Book and its maps served a principal role in shaping discussion on borders by the American plenipotentiaries.[3] He refers to the document as the key source for the American negotiating position on European border proposals. More recent scholarship alludes to the Black Book as the principal document brought to Paris and used in later negotiations regarding territorial questions at the peace conference.[4] Despite being mentioned in many works on the Paris Peace Conference, no previous scholarly investigation has ever thoroughly investigated the Black Book, despite its stature as perhaps the most important document produced by the American Inquiry and used by negotiators at the Paris Peace Conference.[5] Likewise, no studies comprehensively explore the provisions of the Black Book and their impact on the Paris peace treaties.

Many copies of the Black Book were lost in the years immediately following the Paris Peace Conference, with others difficult to access. Copies traveled back to the United States with delegation members and were since lost, while official copies housed at the National Archives remained classified long after the treaties were signed. The original manuscript copy of the Black Book with hand-inked border proposals, housed in the Isaiah Bowman Papers at Johns Hopkins University, remained sealed to most researchers until the 1980s, and only a handful of persons have viewed it since. The first scholar to comprehensively study the American Inquiry's body of work, Lawrence Gelfand, notes that the Black Book remains "the central statement of the work of the Inquiry and its contribution to the Peace Treaty."[6] The influence of this report is clear, as "Wilson had largely made up his mind to accept the recommendations of the Inquiry over those of other elements in his administration."[7] Through his work as lead author, Isaiah Bowman remains clearly one of the most influential advisors on setting the U.S. positions at the peace conference.[8] No successive American geographer has exercised so much influence on pressing U.S. foreign policy decisions.

The Black Book remains of interest particularly for its many maps. Geoffrey Martin recounts the importance of these in his biography of Inquiry geographer and chief cartographer Mark Jefferson:

> Picture the Big Four at Paris lying prone in Mr. Wilson's parlor on a 2 millionth map of Europe till Mr. Lloyd George jumped up and asked for the little black bible of the Americans containing the same things on the scale allowing each map to be reproduced as a 7" × 11" sheet. The large map is too unmanageable.[9]

This description illustrates the utility that the Black Book served. Originally top secret and only held by a few people, the American plenipotentiaries—Inquiry leaders such as Bowman, Miller and Mezes, and a few others—the Black Book was soon seen by other noteworthies. British Prime Minister Lloyd George and the other Big Four members obviously saw Wilson's copy, as he used the maps in discussions with them regarding the new borders being drawn. By late in the conference, it is believed that copies made their way into the hands of non-American delegations. The British are known to have at least one, but how many fell into other foreign hands remains a mystery. Despite this, few of its maps have been reproduced since the 1920s, or received much attention, until now.

The authors of the Black Book clearly understood their materials were anything but perfect. In the opening portions of the book, the scholars introduce the materials:

> Our instructions were, in presenting recommendations, to be definite and set forth the best judgment we could attain at the moment. Naturally our confidence in the conclusions presented varies greatly. Our understanding is that the recommendations presented are to serve as points of departure for the Commission.[10]

The drafters could little imagine how many of their recommendations would be forwarded by President Wilson to other members of the Big Four and often adopted in almost the manner initially presented. Despite its flaws, the Black Book's value as a clear and concise guide to territorial problems made it invaluable to the American negotiators. Indeed, the top secret Black Book can be seen as the principal blueprint for the ensuing peace treaties.

Even though the Black Book proved invaluable at the Paris Peace talks, the Black Book's relevance was not guaranteed because the world underwent tremendous change as it was drafted. Indeed, this was an exceptionally difficult time to compose terms for the upcoming conference, with the rapid shifting of events following the German armistice in November 1918. Austria-Hungary collapsed, as did the Ottoman Empire. The final outcome of the Russian Civil War between the Bolsheviks and the imperialists remained unclear, and events throughout the Balkans were tenuous at best. However, the terms of the German armistice were clear, as they solely focused on Wilson's peace program. The Inquiry had been central to the crafting of these points, but much had altered in the intervening three months prior to the start of the peace conference. Even before the armistice was signed, some of the geographic points had become moot. For example, Point

X, which read, "The peoples of Austria-Hungary, whose place among the nations we wish to see safeguarded and assured, should be accorded the freest opportunity to autonomous development,"[11] an obviously outdated statement. Minority populations throughout the Empire were demanding outright independence by October 1918.[12] Autonomous development within Austria-Hungary was an unrealistic goal by the time the Black Book was in development due to the dramatic turn of events with the declaration of independence by the Czechoslovaks and further calls for the dissolution of the dual monarchy. All the major powers in Central and Eastern Europe were disintegrating, and new national councils had emerged in the power vacuum.[13] The Inquiry scholars had to take such changes into account in their territorial suggestions, rather than just preparing peace proposals based purely on the Fourteen Points. American plenipotentiary General Tasker Bliss noted:

> A change in an existing frontier may be demanded for either two general reasons:
>
> 1) It is *right*, from the point of view of the interests of the peoples immediately concerned, to do so;
> 2) It is *expedient*, from the point of view of the interests of the world at large, to do so.[14]

The difference between these competing claims would come up again and again in Paris. While Bliss' first point resonates with Wilsonian principles, the competing pressures of time and the need to get a final settlement in place often ran up against the vision of the Fourteen Points. It was in the Austro-Hungarian context that these proposals would have to veer the furthest from the Points (see Figure 2.1), but in many areas where borders were in contention, the Inquiry would shape new proposals that took into account more than just the points, as will be seen in the coming chapters.

The maps presented in the Black Book and other reports provide a clear picture of the Wilsonian program at Paris. Isaiah Bowman guided this project and relied heavily on Mark Jefferson, his chief cartographer, to produce the accompanying maps. Jefferson assembled a cartographic team that could take advantage of new drafting and printing technologies to rapidly produce a huge cartographic collection for the

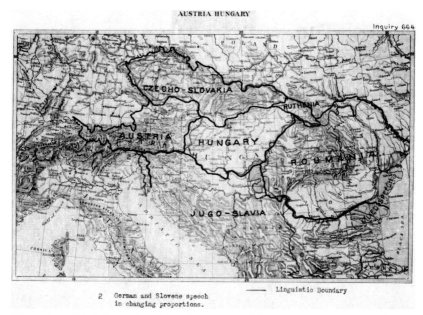

Figure 2.1. *Black Book Map of Austria-Hungary: This map proposes a series of states to replace the Austro-Hungarian Empire. Many final borders set in this region at the Paris Peace Conference coincide fairly closely to those in the Black Book, although this map interestingly also proposes an independent Ruthenia, a region that has never been an independent state. (Map from JHU Bowman Papers MS 58 13.13)*

American delegation. Inquiry members were sent to Europe to gather data for this project and to meet with other Allied preparatory commissions to see what cartographic work they were engaged in.[15] This project came to dominate American preparations in the final months of the Inquiry, when the Black Book was collated. Simon Mezes reflected on this cartographic project after the conference ended:

> Base maps were constructed for the whole of Europe and the Near East, and for various sections of the continent that would surely be involved in the settlements of the Conference. In volume this was one of the largest undertakings of The Inquiry, and it did have educative value for its staff, aiding, as it did, toward an understanding of the most contentious regions the Conference had to consider.[16]

Many people involved in this mapping program would serve in Paris on territorial commissions that set the borders in the various peace treaties.

ties. In many cases, the Inquiry proposed borders hewed closely with those established in the treaties. In the end, the vast majority of Inquiry reports on Europe, and the vast majority of the Black Book, focused on postwar boundaries and the creation of new states in Eastern Europe. Many of these maps clearly reflect the cartographic prowess of the Inquiry members. They illuminate factors beyond just language that would come to play an important role in the discussions over certain frontiers, such as those in the South Tyrol (see Figure 2.2).

Not only border proposal maps, but also ethnographic maps, were produced in the Inquiry reports. Although not contained within the Black Book, these maps were often used along with the Black Book by the plenipotentiaries. These maps often frame the problems approached in Inquiry reports as ones of race and territory. In separating nationalities by international borders, the Inquiry reports and the Black Book, especially, suggest that such divisions would lead to a lasting peace. These maps, however, also point to the problems inherent in drawing such lines. When viewing Eastern European ethnographic maps, it looks as if one is peering through a kaleidoscope, making the task of boundary drawing particularly challenging, as a reasonable frontier is virtually impossible to discern. This challenge was further compounded by trying to determine national sympathy; languages and religions did not always give an accurate indication as to which nationality a particular group of people belonged to. This became the foremost geopolitical problem encountered at the Paris Peace Conference.[17] Conflicts over what factor defines a nation remain flashpoints even today, especially in regions like the Balkans and the Middle East.

Along with the Black Book, the less often mentioned Red Book was also presented to the American plenipotentiaries. It focused on the problems of the colonial world beyond Europe and the Middle East. This final report, along with the earlier reports by the Inquiry, lacks the rigor or attention devoted to the problems in the Black Book. The Inquiry's efforts in this area were hurt by a lack of qualified experts in higher education, due primarily to a lack of academic interest in regions such as Africa, Asia, and the Pacific. Two factors demonstrate why this is not surprising: 1) Eurocentrism and racism were well established within the Academy, and 2) the United States held no colonies in these regions and thus the principal region outside the "civilized" world

Plate IV. Map showing coincidence of proposed new frontier with northern limit of the Adige geographic basin (shaded blue). While the upper Eisack basin drains into the Adige through a long, narrow gorge below Klausen, the upper basin is in reality more open toward the German areas north and east.

━━━━━ Divide between Adige system of connecting trenches on the south, and the Inn and Drave systems on the north; also the proposed new frontier.

━━━━━ Hydrographic divide , the 1915 Treaty of London line , and the best strategic frontier.

•••••••• Present Austro-Italian frontier.

Figure 2.2. *Basin Map of the South Tyrol: This map from the Black Book compares the American and Treaty of London proposals for the border between Italy and Austria. The map supports taking the American proposed line, further to the south, so that watershed basins and other physical landforms conform to the border. This style of border justification fits in well with geographic understandings of the time, defining "natural regions" as appropriate for maintaining political unity. (Map from JHU Bowman Papers MS 58 13.13)*

that received attention in the American Academy was Latin America, likely due to factors such as the Monroe Doctrine and perhaps merely its proximity. Nothing on Latin America would come up in Paris, as the defeated powers possessed no colonies there, and indeed even the victorious powers governed little territory in the Western Hemisphere. This was very different when considering non-European areas of the Eastern Hemisphere. Germany had colonial holdings in Africa and the Pacific, along with considerable influence in China, particularly around the port of Tsingdao (hence why this city remains the producer of China's most famous beer). However, colonial issues remained nothing more than a footnote at the Paris Peace Conference, with little said regarding them in the Fourteen Points and little time devoted by the Big Four to colonial issues outside the Middle East. Not only did colonial areas receive little attention, but self-determination was not considered as a factor in dealing with the colonies. Rather, colonies ended up being traded between European powers.

Despite this, the Inquiry did show influence in the disposition of certain colonies through the creation of the mandate system. It is Inquiry member George Lewis Beer that proposed the idea of mandates, which gained the support of all American plenipotentiaries except Secretary of State Lansing.[18] The mandate system would be applied later to the Ottoman territories gained by Britain and France. These areas would sit under the control of a Great Power, but in concert with the League of Nations and with the understanding that these areas would be prepared for eventual self-government and independence. This Inquiry-originated idea would later influence the creation of the United Nations Trusteeship Council and the establishment of the Trust Territories after World War II. Unlike at the Paris Peace Conference, the United States would acquire some of these territories at this later date, eventually relinquishing them to full independence in the 1990s, something that never happened for many World War I mandates such as Palestine, which remained in British hands until after World War II.

The creation of the Black and Red Books stands out as the most important of the Inquiry's accomplishments. Following their creation, the work of the Inquiry was practically over, as these marked the end of the research phase for the organization.[19] These reports clearly would influence the final treaties in many ways, as will be seen. Despite this prolific output, it was the base maps themselves, along with the border proposal maps that served the delegation best. Simon Mezes notes how few of the other Inquiry maps were used in Paris:

> But at the Conference these maps were hardly used at all. Some of the cases containing them were not opened. The world series millionth maps proved to be sufficient for all needs. They constituted a sort of international currency, readily accessible, familiar to all participants, and inexpensive.[20]

This is confirmed by the frequent mention of these maps in meeting notes from the Big Four.

The Inquiry's task in creating these guidelines was incredibly difficult. The United States only entered the war in 1917, thus giving the Inquiry only about one year to prepare for the peace. Inquiry leaders strove for high quality reports, often facing a lack of time and resources to meet the standards they set. Other than the colored books, most of these reports went unused by the American plenipotentiaries since most of these reports "contained few well-conceived, systematic plans for peace."[21] The Inquiry realized it would play a major role in the conference. Through their reports and technical assistance, the Inquiry prepared to aid the American delegation in two ways:

1. By closely analyzing and defining the issues and expressing them in the terms in which statesmen think.
2. By supplying a well-organized body of critical data which will vitalize the principles laid down by the parties in agreement and help in carrying them out.[22]

They little realized that the experts were in for much more, with figures such as Isaiah Bowman and David Hunter Miller serving key roles in the special committees and working as American diplomats, rather than just technical advisors. Despite what some would call the redundant earlier work of the Inquiry, it will become clear that the top secret Black Book stands out, not only for its influence on the final peace, but also in the Wilsonian vision that it presents, especially in areas where the American plan did not make it onto the world map.

Figure 2.3. *Isaiah Bowman and International Experts in Paris: Bowman, front row second from left, is seen gathering with other territorial experts from around the globe in the opening days of the Paris Peace Conference. (JHU Bowman Papers MS 58)*

NOTES

1. Two copies of this report have been consulted for this research. The manuscript copy is held at Johns Hopkins University (Bowman Papers Series MS 58 Box 13.13) and one of the printed versions has been bound with the diary of David Hunter Miller at the U.S. Department of State Library (see Miller 1924 in the bibliography). For more on these primary source materials, see the discussion on them in the bibliography.

2. Black Book Pg. 2.

3. Sidney Mezes. 1921. "Preparations for Peace," in *What Really Happened at Paris: The Story of the Peace Conference, 1918–1919 by American Delegates*, ed. Edward House. New York: Charles Scribner's Sons.

4. Geoffrey Martin. 1968. *Mark Jefferson: Geographer*. Ypsilanti, MI: Eastern Michigan University Press; Walworth, Arthur. 1986. *Wilson and His Peacemakers: American Diplomacy at the Paris Peace Conference, 1919*. New York: W.W. Norton and Company; Neil Smith. 2003. *American Empire: Roosevelt's Geographer and the Prelude to Globalization*. Berkeley: University of California Press; Jeremy Crampton. 2006. "The Cartographic Calculation of Space: Race Mapping and the Balkans at the Paris Peace Conferece of 1919." *Social and Cultural Geography* (7:5).

5. Crampton 2006.

6. Lawrence Gelfand. 1963. *The Inquiry: American Preparations for Peace 1917–1919*. New Haven: Yale University Press. Pg. 182.

7. David Andelman. 2008. *A Shattered Peace: Versailles 1919 and the Price We Pay Today*. Hoboken, NJ: John Wiley & Sons. Pg. 271.

8. Smith 2003.

9. Martin 1968, Pg. 184. From a letter from Mark Jefferson to Alfred Meyer, written some thirty years after the Paris Peace Conference.

10. Black Book Pg. 4.

11. Address of President Wilson to Congress, January 8, 1918. In Arthur Link. *The Papers of Woodrow Wilson, Volume 45*. Princeton: Princeton University Press, 1984. Pg. 536.

12. Bullitt Lowry. 1996. *Armistice 1918*. Kent, OH: Kent State Press.

13. David Turnock. 1989. *Eastern Europe: An Historical Geography 1815–1945*. London: Routledge.

14. General Tasker Bliss to the Secretary of State. FRUS Vol. I, Pg. 294–296.

15. Gelfand 1963.

16. Mezes 1921, Pg. 5.

17. Crampton 2006.

18. Gelfand 1963.

19. Mezes 1921.

20. Mezes 1921, Pg. 5.

21. Gelfand 1963. Pg. 314.

22. Relation of the Work of the Inquiry to the Peace Conference. JHU Bowman Papers MS 58 13.3.

CHAPTER 3

Negotiating Borders Part 1—A Survey of Boundaries Drawn in 1919 That Survive Today

Although much scholarship has focused on the so-called failings of the Paris Peace Conference, much of the map drawn following World War I remains with us to this very day. The United States brought many border proposals to the table that were adopted at the conference and have survived to this day without modification. Not only did these new borders maintain staying power throughout a century of massive political tumult and re-drawings of the world map, but they did so in many cases in areas that witnessed other borders shift massively, with many new states emerging. The new borders of Western and Central Europe would prove to have the longest staying power, but some borders proposed and later drawn in Eastern Europe have also survived to the present day. During the Second World War, many of these disappeared temporarily as Nazi Germany expanded and annexed most of the European continent, but at war's end, they were restored to their post–World War I lines.

To fairly judge the American plan for peace, it is necessary to look closely at the long-standing legacy of the conference as seen through the borders that remain with us today.

THE WESTERN FRONTIERS OF GERMANY

One year prior to the armistice, Germany stood as the most powerful state in all of Europe, and perhaps the world. In early 1918, Germany signed the Treaty of Brest-Litovsk with Lenin and the Bolsheviks of Russia, relieving the German army of a two-front conflict and granting

Germany, temporarily, occupation over a massive amount of eastern territory in modern-day Poland, Lithuania, Latvia, Estonia, Belarus and Ukraine. These victories were short-lived, as Germany found itself desperately seeking an armistice by the end of the same year. Germany would confront changes in three directions through the treaties, dramatically shrinking it from its post–Brest-Litovsk borders and even quite significantly from its pre–World War I boundary.

The western borders of Germany underwent a significant change at war's end, with Germany losing territory to both Belgium and France. Woodrow Wilson specifically called for these changes in his Fourteen Points speech:

> VII. Belgium, the whole world will agree, must be evacuated and restored, without any attempt to limit the sovereignty which she enjoys in common with all other free nations. No other single act will serve as this will serve to restore confidence among the nations in the laws which they have themselves set and determined for the government of their relations with one another. Without this healing act the whole structure and validity of international law is forever impaired.
>
> VIII. All French territory should be freed and the invaded portions restored, and the wrong done to France by Prussia in 1871 in the matter of Alsace-Lorraine, which has unsettled the peace of the world for nearly fifty years, should be righted, in order that peace may once more be made secure in the interest of all.[1]

The conflict on the western front had after all begun with Germany's invasion of Belgium, thus restoration was the logical first step, taking place as soon as the armistice was signed in 1918. However, the specific border changes made in Paris extended beyond restoration of Germany's 1913 borders. Wilson specifically called for the return of Alsace and Lorraine to France, two regions that France lost in the Franco-Prussian War. Returning these regions was called for despite their significant ethnic German majorities. In the end, the adopted settlement on the western border was one that Germany had already agreed to prior to the start of the actual conference.[2] Two factors were central to setting Germany's new western border: 1) justice to local populations despite Germany's crimes, and 2) satisfaction of the well-founded demands of Germany's neighbors.

Resolving the issue of Alsace-Lorraine through the peace settlement was a top priority given the position it held in the Black Book; Alsace-Lorraine is the first portion of the peace proposal within the Inquiry's policy recommendations. The Black Book called for the entirety of Alsace and Lorraine to be returned to France, including areas of Lorraine that were annexed into the German Saar region in 1814. The Black Book recommended the demilitarization of areas on the German side of the Franco-German frontier, an idea echoed by the French.

The regions of Alsace and Lorraine had been in French sight since their loss in 1871. They were so central to the French demands for terms of the final settlement that Alsace and Lorraine were ceded to France in the armistice of 1918; the Treaty of Versailles merely ratified the transfer. However, the exact border had to be determined at the peace conference.

The neighboring region of the Saar was discussed similarly, and unlike Alsace-Lorraine, would prove complex to solve, due to its strong German character. The French coveted the Saar because of its large coal deposits (also extensive in Alsace-Lorraine), along with other strategic mineral resources. However, Wilsonian principles do not consider economic issues, making it especially difficult to deal with a region that showed very little affinity for France.

Not only did the Black Book call for transferring Alsace-Lorraine to the French, but also two portions of Germany were recommended for transfer to Belgium (see Figure 3.1). The Inquiry further suggested that the regions around the towns of Malmedy and Eupen be transferred. Principally, the Inquiry was concerned that the important Belgian industrial center of Liege sat within the range of German artillery, thus necessitating a buffer zone. French-speaking Walloons (one of Belgium's main ethnic groups) populated the area near Malmedy, thus making this change in line with the Wilsonian principle of placing people within their nation-state. However, the other ceded areas were principally German in population.

Belgium's position as victim of German aggression at the war's start was central to the proposal of extending the hinterlands around Eupen and Malmedy. Writing after the war, Isaiah Bowman noted, "The World War saw Belgium afflicted by the most grievous of long succession of servitudes and disasters."[3] Belgium's strategic location as the most direct route between Germany and France caused such problems that, only by

The black line indicates a possible Strategic

Rectification of the Prussian frontier.

Figure 3.1. *Black Book Border Proposal for Belgium: The Inquiry recommended that Belgium's eastern border extend into formerly German territory around the cities of Eupen and Malmedy (see black line for the new "strategic frontier"). For the most part, this new territory was linguistically and ethnically German, but the Inquiry was strongly influenced by past events, rather than the principle of self-determination, in crafting this proposal. (Map from JHU Bowman Papers MS 58 13.13)*

gaining a larger amount of territory, was it believed that Belgium could defend itself and its key eastern cities from future German aggression.

The border changes proposed for both France and Belgium defied the ethno-linguistic principles that President Wilson had enunciated. German-speaking populations were to be transferred from Germany to neighboring French-speaking places. In the case of Alsace-Lorraine, there were significant French-speaking minorities. French speakers accounted for approximately 500,000 in Alsace-Lorraine, of a total population of around 1.8 million.[4] The two areas gained by Belgium also removed German-speaking areas from the German state. Belgium's acquisition of the hinterlands around Eupen added over 50,000 people, mostly German speaking, while the area around Malmedy added close to 10,000 people, mostly French-speaking.[5] Thus, the Malmedy acquisition stood in line with the principles espoused by Wilson, while the other areas Germany ceded in the west were transferred for reasons other than self-determination.

Unlike the enormous controversies encountered over many boundary negotiations at the peace conference, the transfers to Belgium and France were handled with ease. In the notes of the Council of Four, only rarely do references to Alsace-Lorraine appear, and these almost wholly examine how reparations in the area would be handled. The final Treaty of Versailles recognized French sovereignty over Alsace-Lorraine from November 11, 1918.[6]

As for the Belgian territory, the final transfer granted less land to Belgium than envisioned in the American peace plan. The new Belgian boundaries were entirely laid out in the Commission on Belgian and Danish Affairs—an experts' panel composed of mid-ranking diplomats—rather than in discussions among the Big Four. The Inquiry's Dr. Simon Mezes represented the United States in the Commission, where they unanimously agreed the zones around both should be voted upon via plebiscite. The commission provided the following as justification for the transfer of Eupen and Malmedy, as long as the final treaty provided a means for consulting the local population:

> [T]his region has continued in close economic and social relations with the adjacent portions of Belgium, and in spite of a century of Prussification the Walloon speech has maintained itself among several thousand of its inhabitants.[7]

Although the Inquiry proposed a larger area, in discussion with the other Great Powers on the commission (France, the United Kingdom, Italy and Japan), it was decided that the treaty would transfer these two areas only under the condition that each would hold votes under the auspices of the League of Nations. Another area of one square mile, the unpopulated and wooded Neutral Morosenet, which had been ill-defined in the 1815 treaty between Belgium and Prussia was also transferred to the Belgians. In the end, the Treaty of Versailles did not call for an actual plebiscite, but rather:

> During the six months after the coming into force of this Treaty, registers will be opened by the Belgian authority at Eupen and Malmedy in which the inhabitants of the above territory will be entitled to record in writing a desire to see the whole or part of it remain under German sovereignty.[8]

Both areas opened these registers in 1920, under the auspices of the Belgian government and only 271 people, out of over 33,000 participating, voted to keep these areas within Germany.[9] Clearly, by conducting this exercise without international supervision, the Belgians compelled a result that could not be described as democratic under any fair consideration. Despite this, the two regions only returned to German hands for the period of the German occupation of Belgium during World War II. Since then, they have been a part of Belgium, with Eupen serving as the principal city for the German-speaking community of Belgium, a government-recognized minority community within the state. This type of minority recognition clearly fit within the protections for minorities that were also key to the Wilsonian peace program.

Other border proposals were more draconian in their impact on Germany than those finally adopted. France initially proposed annexing all of the Saar and creating a new state in the Rhineland. Only through the promise of a fifteen-year occupation and defense guarantees from the United Kingdom and the United States would they relent on their proposal.[10] A compromise was reached that demilitarized the Rhineland and called for a plebiscite for Saarland.

The Inquiry recognized France had some claims to the Saar region. In the Black Book, the Inquiry noted that under certain narrow circumstances, France should be granted a large portion of the Saarland:

If the disarmament of the German territory on the left bank of the Rhine is disapproved, the protection to France that was intended to effect may have to be security by pushing her frontier in the valley of the Saar beyond the line of 1814 so as to include most of the remainder of the basin of the Saar.[11]

The Big Four unanimously supported disarming the Rhineland. This negated a need, in the view of the American peace planners, for a new boundary. Discussions on the Saar region began early in their meetings. The French proposed the Saar region be ceded to France along with Alsace-Lorraine, although this was opposed by the other powers. The French justified their claims on need for the coal deposits.[12] It was clear, even to the Americans, that resources would play a large role in the discussions of these borders, as the Black Book map of the area denotes the resources, including the vast coal deposits of the Saar, which did indeed dominate French discussion in the Big Four. By early April, three separate proposals were in play: 1) to keep the Saar under German sovereignty but to transfer local administration to France, 2) to transfer sovereignty of the Saar to the League of Nations under French administration, or 3) to establish a separate Saar state under French protection.[13]

Discussions of the Saar and how to deal with the Rhineland stretched from January until May, when the French agreed to a compromise: Germany would demilitarize the entire left bank of the Rhine River and France would gain temporary control of the Saar. However, the Treaty of Versailles mandated fifteen years of French control before a plebiscite was to be conducted, under the auspices of the League of Nations. The treaty did call for France to retain access to the coalfields, even if Germany regained the territory at that time.[14] In 1935, 90.3 percent of the population voted to join Germany, 8.8 percent voted to maintain the League of Nations mandate, and only 0.4 percent voted to join France, thus terminating the French mandate over the region.[15] The results clearly demonstrated the people of the Saar held a strong affinity for Germany, as also evidenced by the fact that almost the entire population spoke German, and thus the final dispensation of the region was clearly in line with the principle of self-determination as espoused in the American program for peace.

The German treaty made major revisions on the western frontiers of the state (see Figure 3.2). The transfers of territory to both Belgium and France remain as the modern borders between these states and Germany. However, both the Saar mandate and the demilitarization of the Rhineland did not last long. By the mid-1930s, the rise of Nazi Germany and the victory by Germany in the Saar plebiscite led to the negation of these two provisions of the Treaty of Versailles.

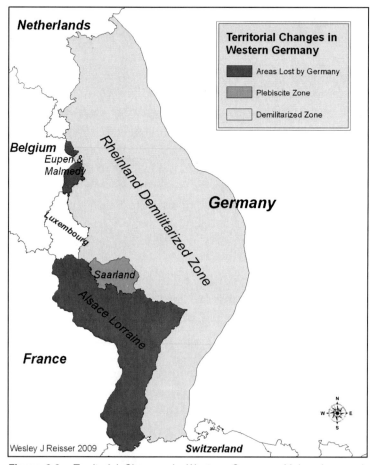

Figure 3.2. *Territorial Changes in Western Germany: Major changes in Germany's frontiers were affected by the Treaty of Versailles. Those that permanently transferred territory to France and Belgium remain as the international borders today, while the arrangements for the Saar and the Rhineland (Rheinland in German) demilitarized zone lasted fifteen years. (Cartography by the author)*

Following the war, large numbers of ethnic Germans resided outside of German territory, including 1.5 million in France and about 115,000 in Belgium, according to German sources at the time.[16] The losses in the west were ethnic and economic with regard to Alsace-Lorraine and the Saar, while mostly strategic with Eupen and Malmedy. The settlements clearly stretched beyond rectifying borders based solely on national self-determination. However, these western borders have stood the test of time and are close to those proposed by the American Inquiry. Due to the circumstances in play at the time of the Paris Peace Conference, and due to the American commitment to return Alsace-Lorraine to France, it is not surprising that the American program introduced at the conference was not based on ethno-linguistic grounds, but rather on strategic ones concerning these particular boundaries.

THE SCHLESWIG PLEBISCITE—
DEMOCRATIC BORDER-MAKING

Schleswig, the southern portion of the Jutland Peninsula (the shared region between Germany and Denmark), would prove a much easier border to resolve following the war than those along the western borders of Germany. Denmark remained neutral throughout the conflict, but when analyzing Germany's borders, it became clear to the Inquiry that revision was necessary along the Danish-German border. The Schleswig region had been in dispute between Prussia and Denmark since 1864, and in the 1866 Treaty of Prague, a plebiscite was called for to determine the border, with a date for the vote to be determined later.[17] The Treaty of Prague's Article V proposed the plebiscite, and on November 23, 1918, President Wilson affirmed his support for this course of action.[18] The population of Schleswig was mixed, with both Danish and German speakers, and a gradient from denser Danish concentrations in the north to greater German concentrations in the south.

The Inquiry adopted the proposal first suggested in the 1860s, by again calling for a plebiscite (see Figure 3.3). Their plan for Schleswig recommended:

That the northern districts of Schleswig be ceded to Denmark, if a plebiscite shows that the people wish to be united to Denmark.[19]

Figure 3.3. *Map of Schleswig Plebiscite Zones: The Peace Conference adopted lines for the Schleswig plebiscite based on those laid out in the Black Book. A series of large format maps were finally prepared to denote the zones for the final vote, based upon the Black Book proposed zones. (Cartography by the author)*

Most of the borders proposed at Paris were drawn entirely by outsiders, but Schleswig would prove significantly different. The Inquiry broke the territory into districts moving from the north to the south, such that each could conduct a plebiscite, with the furthest north going first. Once an area chose to remain in Germany, the plebiscite would not move further south, so as to avoid creating non-contiguous territories. This plan would thus allow areas of Danish affinity the opportunity to join with Denmark without transferring regions wishing to remain within Germany.

The Sunday after the armistice, November 17, a large meeting was held in northern Schleswig where the Danish population called for the right to a plebiscite to determine whether their region should remain in

Germany or be transferred to Denmark.[20] The Committee on Belgian and Danish Affairs at the Paris Peace Conference was assigned the duty to devise a solution to this. Little controversy existed among the Great Powers, and it was quickly resolved that the plebiscite plan would go forward for Schleswig.[21] The Germans objected to this procedure, but the Schleswig plebiscite easily made its way into the Treaty of Versailles, which defined the zones for the plebiscite. In 1920, the plebiscite was organized under the auspices of the League of Nations (unlike that held in Eupen and Malmedy), wherein the northern zone voted 74 percent in favor for union with Denmark, while a few weeks later the second zone voted overwhelmingly in favor of remaining in Germany.[22]

The Schleswig example provided the first test case for a true plebiscite after the First World War. Based on Wilsonian parameters, nothing could measure a population's own self-determination better than having them vote to determine which country they wished to reside in. Unlike later plebiscites, such as the one in the Saar, where outside influence and Great Power politics played a major role, the Schleswig plebiscite was carried out as envisioned. The boundary remains in place today exactly where it was delimited from the plebiscite, and it remains a model example of how to use democratic tools in the demarcation of territory.

CREATING RUMP AUSTRIA

Inquiry geographer Leon Dominian described Austria-Hungary as a "seething reservoir of nationalities."[23] In addition to the dominant German and Hungarian populations, Austria-Hungary contained substantial numbers of other peoples. The Germans and Hungarians each represented about ten million people in the Empire; however, they were outnumbered by about 20 million Slavic speakers (including Czechs, Slovaks, Serbs, Croats and Slovenes) and several million Romance speakers (primarily Romanians and Italians).[24] Immediately following the outbreak of the war, many in Austria-Hungary already saw its demise nearing. The Austro-Hungarian Empire survived into the 20th century mainly through artificial measures and control of the Danube River corridor.[25] However, the Empire clearly failed to build institutions or concepts that would create widespread enthusiasm for the state, as evidenced by further agitation for devolution of authority after the creation of the dual monarchy in 1867.

During the lead-up to the peace conference, many American diplomats wearied of dismantling Austria-Hungary. However, members of the Inquiry advanced the claims of the Italians, Slavs and Romanians for liberation from the Empire. The Black Book plan provided for Austria-Hungary's dismemberment into several constituent states including Czechoslovakia, Ruthenia, Yugoslavia and Romania (see Figure 2.1). In the end, Austria lost all but 32,000 of 116,000 square miles of its territory in the Treaty of St. Germain.[26]

Throughout Eastern Europe, territorial claims were derived from those of defunct empires and kingdoms (such as Roman Dacia and the medieval Kingdom of Serbia), along with a variety of other factors which led to groups producing multiple overlapping claims to territory.[27] Claims and counterclaims proliferated both before and at the conference, leaving the Big Four in a difficult position to determine where the final borders would lie. In the case of Austria, this was especially complex, due to the massive amount of re-bordering that took place in Central Europe over the preceding centuries. Austria had never really existed as a state for the German speakers of the Hapsburg realms, but had always been a multiethnic entity under a German-speaking royal family. Austrians lacked a separate national consciousness, and the new Austria would emerge as a state, but not a nation.[28]

The new Austrian state would find itself in possession of a dramatically reduced territory, even by the standards of the vanquished states. As such, Austria, once the largest state in the world (when the Hapsburgs also controlled Spain and its various New World colonies), ended up as one of Europe's smaller states and one of the smallest states to emerge out of the Austro-Hungarian Empire. Not only would the new Austria be landlocked, but it would in effect consist of the capital of the Empire, Vienna, and the German-speaking hinterlands of the city, along with Alpine German areas of the Empire to the west of Vienna, while losing many German-speaking areas to the east along with all other regions that had long been under Vienna's control.

The dismantling of Austria was not set in stone when the Inquiry began work on creating plans for the peace. Woodrow Wilson did not call for any specific remedy for the Austro-Hungarian Empire in his Fourteen Points, rather in Point X, Wilson called for :

The peoples of Austria-Hungary, whose place among the nations we wish to see safeguarded and assured, should be accorded the freest opportunity to autonomous development.[29]

Wilson did not specify the breakup of the Empire, but rather called for assurances that each of the Empire's ethnic groups be granted the ability to develop autonomously. However, as preparations for peace progressed, the situation in Europe changed dramatically. Subject nationalities of the Hapsburgs began declaring independence in the final days prior to the armistice, starting with Czechoslovakia on October 28. Prior to the armistice on November 11, 1918, the Austrian government requested a separate armistice along the lines of the Fourteen Points, with minor modifications. Secretary of State Lansing replied to the Austrians that the tenth point no longer was considered valid in its original form by the United States:

> Since that sentence was written and uttered to the Congress of the United States, the Government of the United States has recognized that a state of belligerency exists between the Czechoslovaks and the German and Austro-Hungarian Empires and that the Czechoslovak National Council is a de facto belligerent Government clothed with proper authority to direct the military and political affairs of the Czechoslovaks. It has also recognized in the fullest manner the justice of the nationalistic aspirations of the Jugo-slavs for freedom.
>
> The President is, therefore, no longer at liberty to accept the mere "autonomy" of these peoples as a basis of peace, but is obliged to insist that they, and not he, shall be the judges of what action on the part of the Austro-Hungarian Government will satisfy their aspirations and their conception of their rights and destiny as members of the family of nations.[30]

By the start of the conference, it was clear that there was no way to put Austria-Hungary back together.

As the final plans were organized for the American delegation, it was determined that a series of states—not just Czechoslovakia and Yugoslavia—would emerge out of the Hapsburg Empire. For Austria itself, the Black Book called for the creation of a rump state similar to the state created at the conference:

> The frontiers of the future state of Austria, if Austria chooses the path of independence, are drawn on the map so as to correspond roughly to the

central block of Germans living in the crownlands of Upper and Lower Austria, Salzburg, Carinthia, the Voralberg, German Tyrol, and Styria.

Except upon the Italian and Jugo-Slav frontier, the historic boundaries separating German Austria from Bavaria, Bohemia, Moravia, and Hungary have been preserved. These historic boundaries leave about 2,500,000 Germans in western Hungary, but the adjustment of the frontier to include them would result in a disturbance of long-established institutions, and until it becomes clear that it is sincerely desired by the people in question, it seems unwise to include them.

A similar block of 250,000 Germans is left in Bohemia and Moravia to form a part of the state of Czecko-Slovakia. But the people seem rather to prefer union with the new Czecho-Slovak state, though their sentiments have not yet been clearly enough expressed to form the basis of a positive conclusion. It should likewise be noted once more that there is everywhere a decided disadvantage in disturbing such historic entities as Bohemia and Moravia.

Along the Jugo-Slav frontier, the proposed boundary departs from the language line only so far as is necessary to avoid derangements of economic relations.[31]

The problems of creating such a land-locked state were also considered by the American plan. To allow Austria access to international waterways, the American plan called for the assurances of Austria to ports, either in Italy at Trieste or the proposed Yugoslav port at Fiume, or both.[32]

The American plan was quickly disseminated, and the first territorial commissions were established on February 1, 1919, to deal with the nationalities of the Austro-Hungarian Empire.[33] The commissions focused on the subject nationalities, but with no Austrian or Hungarian commission; rather, these states would end up with whatever was not set aside for the other peoples of Central Europe. Noted historian of the Paris Peace Conference Margaret MacMillan summarizes the views towards the Austrians: "What was fair to Austria and Hungary, according to the principles of self-determination, what was necessary if they were to survive, were questions that caused little concern in Paris."[34] As these commissions went about their work, the final Austrian state came together in a manner that closely reflected that proposed by the American Inquiry experts. The biggest difference occurred in one area along the historic border between Hungary and Austria that was proposed for transfer to Austria, due to its German majority. While this proposed transfer opposed the Black Book proposal, this was nevertheless more in line with the Wilsonian program and the standpoint of self-determination. It should also be noted that mainly due to the communist revolution in Hungary, Austria received a Hungarian strip of territory, making the transfer the only territorial addition given to any of the defeated powers.

Within Austria itself, there was great pessimism that such a small state could survive. In his mission through the lands of Austria-Hungary, American diplomat Archibald Cary Coolidge reported:

> The German Austria of the future (of which Vienna contains about a third of the population) is economically of small resources and incapable of standing alone. Only two courses are possible for it: either union with Germany which is favored by the Socialists not so much for nationalistic reasons as because they believe the socialist cause in Austria would be strengthened by it, or a Danubian confederation. This (according to the speakers) is favored by a majority of the people for sentimental, historical, economic and other reasons.[35]

Austrians were greatly disturbed by the events that led to the creation of their new small state. The French feared a larger German state, and were most concerned about any union between Austria and Germany. However, many Austrians and Germans were equally apprehensive. Austria had always been separate, with unique character that many Austrians feared would be lost if Austria were to join with Germany. For the Germans, the biggest concern was that asking for a union with Austria could further complicate their already difficult position in acquiring a just settlement from the conference. Fairly early in their discussions, the Council of Four agreed the German treaty would specifically prohibit *Anschluss* (the merging of the two states) with Austria. The council agreed to a provision in the Treaty of Versailles that would read:

> Germany acknowledges and will fully respect the independence of Austria within the frontiers established by the present treaty as inalienable, except by consent of the Council of the League of Nations.[36]

As France was to be on the Council, and all League matters were to be determined by unanimity, this was as good as a complete denial of any chance for such a union.

As time went on, the Austrian population clearly began to favor a series of actions that later would lead to the temporary disappearance of their state through a merging with Germany. Based upon ethno-linguistic factors, Austria should have been merged into Germany, rather than created as a separate entity. The sentiment of the time was such to keep this from occurring. However, as the years progressed, support for such a maneuver grew stronger, and in 1938 the Austrian-born Chancellor of Germany, Adolf Hitler, effected the *Anschluss*, whereby Austria merged into Germany. Due to Hitler's total abrogation of the Treaty of Versailles much earlier in his tenure as Chancellor, the abrogation of the prohibition of *Anschluss* came as little surprise. Austria remained a part of Germany through the Second World War, but following that war's end, Austria was re-created on the exact same boundaries as those set in the Treaty of St. Germain. Austria retains those World War I era borders to this day.

THE AUSTRO-ITALIAN BORDER

One particular section of the new Austrian border created especially tense problems among the Big Four in Paris. Italy had been promised a large swath of Austrian territory, the South Tyrol in the Alps that contained not only a large Italian population but also a sizeable German population. South Tyrol, today known as the Trentino-Alto Adige region of Italy, presented the Americans and other great powers at Paris with a formidable challenge in the redrawing of Europe's borders. Prior to the war, the entire Tyrol region formed part of the Austrian-ruled portion of the Austro-Hungarian Empire. At the conference, two competing proposals for Tyrol were placed on the table, one based on nationality and the other based on drawing a "strategic frontier" between Austria and Italy. The difference in the nature of the two parties' claims created a border conflict that proved irreconcilable between the parties.[37]

At the outbreak of World War I Italy remained neutral. Both the Central and Entente Powers attempted to gain Italian cooperation and entry into the war. However, Austria-Hungary feared the Italians would enter against them in an attempt to annex Italian populations outside their borders. Austria promised Italy the Trentino (the southernmost portion of South Tyrol) in exchange for staying out of the war. The Austrian offer would have passed 367,000 Italians and Ladins (a small ethnic group that speaks a Romance language) and 14,000 German speakers to Italy, while maintaining 19,000 Italians and 511,000 German speakers in Austrian Tyrol.[38] This includes the population of the North Tyrol, which was not claimed by Italy and remains in Austria today. This territorial transfer to Italy would have occurred at the war's end. The Italians quickly rejected this offer, as they had far grander designs on the Tyrol.

Through the Treaty of London and with large territorial promises at war's end, the Entente Powers secured Italian entry into the war. The treaty promised Italy the Trentino, all of the Tyrol south of the Brenner Pass, Trieste, the Istrian Peninsula, Dalmatia, and even territory in Turkey (see chapters 4 and 5). These large territorial concessions were the primary reason Italy chose to enter the war.[39] More than anything else, Italy wanted to ensure that it had strong borders to defend against a perceived German threat to the north.[40] As a young country that was politically weak, Italy feared Germany as a geopolitical threat and decided to align with the Entente side. The promised gains, made in secret, in Tyrol remained an important aspect of Italy's war aims.

President Wilson clearly came out against such arrangements as the Treaty of London when he laid out his program for peace in the Fourteen Points. The very first point addressed the Treaty of London and similar arrangements directly:

> I. Open covenants of peace, openly arrived at, after which there shall be no private international understandings of any kind but diplomacy shall proceed always frankly and in the public view.[41]

Wilson had been made aware of the secret Treaty of London at the time the United States joined the war in his consultations with the British and French. He refused to recognize them from the start, and the Inquiry went forward in making peace proposals that did not account for these prior agreements, to which the United States was not party.

Italy's victory over Austria-Hungary owed almost nothing to Italian actions and decisions, but was almost only ensured by the victory of her allies elsewhere. The Italian front was one of the few where Austria made gains during the conflict. Despite Italian failings along their front with Austria, the Italians held on to all of the claims made in the Treaty of London when they arrived at the Paris Peace Conference.

When the Inquiry experts began to investigate the Italian-Austrian frontier in preparation for the peace conference, it became evident that many changes would be necessary to rectify the boundary according to Wilsonian principles. Wilson specifically laid out his position on Italian frontiers in the ninth of his Fourteen Points:

> IX. A readjustment of the frontiers of Italy should be effected along clearly recognizable lines of nationality.[42]

It was widely agreed that the current border was too far to the south.[43] The frontiers that had developed predated the nation-state concept, as Austria held the Tyrol before Italy existed as a state. With the United States not a party to the Treaty of London, the Inquiry set out to establish a different border proposal for the peace conference. The frontier, as it stood, was 400 miles long, with only 60 of those miles coinciding with the linguistic boundary between Italian speakers and others.[44] The 1910 Austrian census affirmed that the South Tyrol was not a homogenous German-speaking area. The entire Tyrolean area (including lands retained by Austria) consisted of 93 percent Germans, 5 percent Ladins and 2 percent Italians.[45] However, this probably understated the Italian population and overstated the Germans, as Germans were the dominant ethnic group in Austria. In the southernmost Trentino region, south of Bozen (now known as Bolzano), the Italians actually formed the dominant group when combined with the Ladins.

The Inquiry studies unequivocally prove that Italians only occupied the southernmost areas of Tyrol, in the Trentino district. However, the Italians based their claim not on nationality, but on "strategic reasons." The Brenner Pass boundary, much further to the north, lies along one of the Alps' high ridgelines, thereby making it a much stronger boundary, according to the dominant boundary hypothesis of the time, laid out by British military geographer Colonel Holdich. Holdich's argument that a high mountain ridge made the best defensible boundary coincided with Italian reasoning. The Italians were aware of President Wilson's Fourteen Points, so publicly they argued that using the watershed limits in the high Alps would form a "natural boundary" for Italy, rather than making the strategic argument to the American delegation. This reasoning did not sit well with the American peace planners.

The Black Book called for a compromise line between the linguistic line and that promised in the secret Treaty of London (see Figures 3.4 and 3.5):

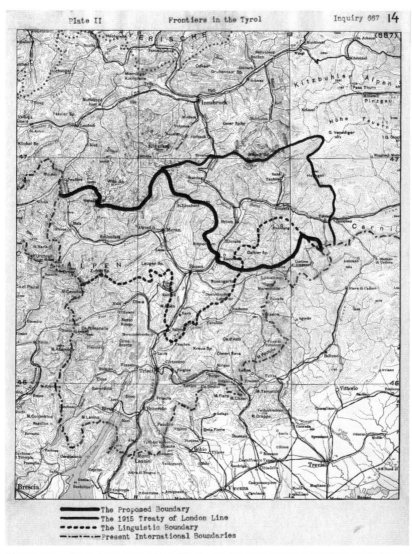

Figure 3.4. *Black Book Map of the Tyrol: The Inquiry proposed the thick black line as the new border between Italy and Austria, while the thinner line represents the Treaty of London line that Italy claimed. Both lay far to the north of the linguistic boundary. (Map from the JHU Bowman Papers MS 58 13.13)*

It is recommended that Italy be given a northern frontier midway between the linguistic line and the line of the treaty of London, 1915. The proposed line is delimited on maps 12 to 15 inclusive.

This recommendation would give Italy all that part of the Tyrol to which she has any just claim on linguistic, cultural or historical grounds.

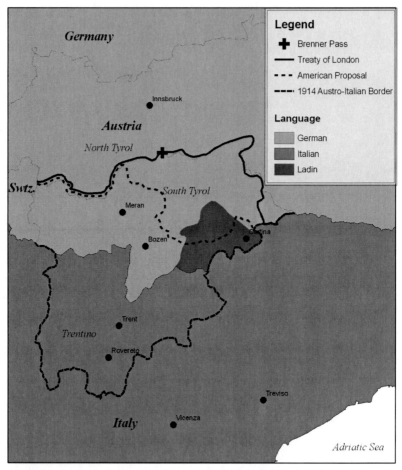

Figure 3.5. *Peace Conference Proposals for the South Tyrol: Both border propos-als give large German-inhabited areas, including the principal German city of Bozen to Italy, although the Treaty of London boundary gives more German-inhabited territory to Italy. The American proposed line divides the small Ladin population between Austria and Italy, thereby disrupting this small ethnic minority more so than the Treaty of London boundary. The Treaty of London line was adopted at the peace conference and remains the border between Austria and Italy today. (Cartography by the author)*

It would leave no rational basis for future irredentist agitation in this direction....

The recommended line does not meet those claims of Italy which are based on strategic grounds alone, for the line of 1915, following as it does the main watershed, gives incomparably the best strategic frontier. On the other hand, the proposed line does ameliorate the intentionally bad frontier imposed upon Italy by Austria, and some such amelioration seems essential if the Italians are to enter a League of Nations with confidence in its ability to render their peaceful existence reasonably sure. The weight of this argument would be augmented if Italy were confronted by a united and potentially powerful German state on the north....

As laid down on the map, the proposed boundary is a good line from the geographical standpoint, since it follows natural lines of demarcation and coincides with the marked topographical barrier between regions climactically dissimilar. Its position is easily recognizable on the ground, it is capable of clear and accurate delimitation, and is not subject to change from natural causes. Since throughout its entire length it traverses regions of little or no population it does not interfere with the activities of the local population, and the small number of practicable passes makes the administration of customs and other frontier regulations simple.

Finally, it is so drawn as to throw into Austria about 71,000 Germans, with a minority of 10,000 Italians and Ladins, forming properly a part of the Austrian realm. Were the line of 1915 to be followed ..., it would simply throw the irredentist problem into Austrian territory and would not lead to a lasting peace.[46]

This went beyond the border that would actually follow Wilsonian principles exactly, but clearly provided a better option in the American view than that proposed by Italy.

The Tyrol region offered one of the simplest places in Europe to draw an ethnographic line, as almost all Germans lived north of the ethnographic divide, while nearly all Italians lived to the south. Despite this, events at the conference coupled with the overall obstinacy of Italy in its territorial demands made a fair settlement practically impossible to achieve. The Black Book states that the 1915 Treaty of London line "gives incomparably the best strategic frontier."[47] Following the highest ground, the Treaty of London line delineates a clear, defensible divide between Italy and Austria. However, despite this, the American proposed line "does ameliorate the intentionally bad frontier imposed upon Italy by Austria."[48]

The American proposal analyzed other border options in South Tyrol. Widespread belief held that the original frontier Austria gained in 1815 was situated too far to the south. Austria dominated the Alpine highlands overlooking Italy, presenting the Italians with a fairly indefensible frontier against the Austrian and German armies to the north. The Inquiry report noted this could be problematic, and was sympathetic to creating a more defensible boundary. They suggested the American-proposed line would render the task of the League of Nations easier by creating a border that would "discourage armed aggression by a powerful German state."[49]

The Americans offered additional rationale to defend their frontier choice over that laid out in the Treaty of London. They considered several geographic factors in delimiting the proposed boundary: it followed a topographical barrier; it separated two dissimilar climactic regions; it could easily be demarcated on the ground; and it traversed an area with little or no population along its entire route.[50]

Although the American line would move 161,000 Germans into Italy, it also kept a significant German population in Austria that under the Treaty of London line would have moved to Italy. Seventy-one thousand Germans along with 10,000 Italians and Ladins would remain in Austria under the proposed line.[51] This compromise on the Treaty of London was meant to appease Austrian concerns that such a large group of German people would be transferred. The report states, "Were the line of 1915 to be followed it would simply throw the irredentist [claims by minorities to have their territory shifted to a neighboring country where they form the majority] problem into Austrian territory and would not lead to a lasting peace."[52] The Italian concerns over having so many of their countrymen in Austria led to their claims on Austrian territory in the first place. However, American experts viewed the Entente Powers' offer of the boundary under the 1915 Treaty of London as overly ambitious. They believed the new border would need to be redrawn to avoid similar complaints from Austria. Little did they know how correct their analysis of the London border would prove to be.

Shortly after the end of hostilities, the U.S. government dispatched Professor A.C. Coolidge to the lands of the Austro-Hungarian Empire to gather a sense on the ground of how peoples would react to the different peace proposals. This was intended to complement the Inquiry's work on the proposed settlements and add an element of ground truth to the overall exercise, as American experts were unable to investigate possible settlements in the field during ongoing hostilities. Coolidge sent several letters and a report to the commissioners' plenipotentiary in Paris regarding the places he visited so his information could be included in their deliberations over the final status of the territories.

Professor Coolidge first reported on the South Tyrol on January 9, 1919, concerned that the German-speaking areas south of the Brenner Pass might be awarded to Italy. He traveled throughout the region meeting with local officials and notables, while also interviewing many local citizens and observing South Tyrol firsthand. Coolidge confirmed that the Bozen district was overwhelmingly German in population, with very few political ties to Italy. He stated, "The Austrians declare that under the principle of self-determination as proclaimed by President Wilson... they do not see how this territory can possibly be taken away from them."[53] He further believed that the Austrians would find the loss of the territory to be an "intolerable injustice."

On March 10, Coolidge presented a final report to the peace conference on the disposition of Austro-Hungarian territories. For the South Tyrol, Coolidge determined:

> The German speaking region of South Tyrol should be given to Austria, not to Italy. All the arguments except perhaps those arising from the political necessities of the present international situation demand that these Tyrolese should remain united with their brethren in the north and not be put under a hated alien rule. History, economic interest and the feelings of the inhabitants are on the same side in this instance... The loss of this beautiful and poetic territory would never be forgiven. The Ladin portion of the Tyrol, although I think that for commercial reasons it would prefer its present affiliation, might be handed over to Italy with less injustice.[54]

This report presented a situation even more tilted toward the Austrian position than either the American proposed line or that of the Treaty of London. These conflicting sets of claims all confronted the Big Four in their deliberations over the fate of South Tyrol.

As negotiations among the Big Four began, Tyrol's situation was one of the first areas given consideration. The Italians, as expected, demanded the entire area as promised under the Treaty of London. As fellow signatories to the treaty, France and Britain also sided in favor of the London line. Word of this quickly filtered out to the Coolidge Mission, and Professor Coolidge hastened a response. In a letter to the commission, he stated, "In no question of boundary at present under discussion have we more clearly the principles of history, nationality and self-determination on one side and strategic and imperialistic considerations on the other... the case might be regarded as test one under the Fourteen Points."[55] He further elaborated that the southern frontier of the German speaking area was perfectly suited for defense and noted this case presented the best coincidence of both a geographical and linguistic boundary.

Coolidge's reports, along with those in the initial American plan, held great sway in the arguments presented by President Wilson. On April 19, 1919, the Big Four met at President Wilson's residence in Paris to discuss the Italian frontiers. President Wilson immediately proposed that the Treaty of London line be disregarded, as the United States was not a signatory to the agreement.[56] The contention made by the Inquiry that the London lines should be voided held resonance in his opening arguments. However, Prime Minister Orlando interjected that Italy should have "natural frontiers" and this meant up to the watershed boundary in the mountains, despite his recognition that non-Italian peoples were included in this claim. President Wilson retorted the peacemakers were trying to make peace on an entirely new basis, thus self-determination attained greater import in consideration than strategic arguments. He was willing to meet most Italian claims, but in the Tyrol there would need to be adjustments.

However, due to problems in other areas of the negotiations, President Wilson acceded to the Italian claim on Tyrol on April 23.[57] The strategic arguments by Italy eventually convinced Wilson that the Brenner Pass frontier should be adopted, despite the President's concerns that Italy would receive such a large German population.[58] Reports out of Tyrol immediately showed despair amongst the local populace that their homeland was to be transferred to Italy.[59] The discussions over Tyrol remained on the agenda on some conference committees until the Treaty of St. Germain was presented to Austria, but with no substantive change in positions. Secretary of State Lansing in May 1919, affirmed that precedence would be given to topographical concerns over ethnographical considerations in regard to the Brenner Pass boundary.[60]

American experts felt great disappointment in how Italy's final borders shaped up, as the new borders extended far beyond the ethnographic frontier all the way from Switzerland to the Adriatic (for a discussion of the Italian-Yugoslav border, see chapter 4).[61] After the war, the Inquiry's chief geographer Isaiah Bowman noted:

We are all agreed that some of the settlements are bad. I personally feel that the settlement in the Tyrol is extremely bad. But for the work of the peace conference was done under conditions wholly new to the statesmen of our time and under great pressure, because the whole world had fallen into disorder.[62]

Despite these problems, the Italian-Austrian border remains in place today. The tensions within the Big Four almost undermined the entire conference. There was a high degree of tension through the 1950s, but with autonomy granted to the region by Italy, the conflict ameliorated, and today there is no contention between the two states over the border—one that has far less meaning now that both Italy and Austria are members of the European Union.

CREATING RUMP HUNGARY

Of the defeated powers, only Hungary would face a greater reduction in land and population in the final settlements than Austria. The Hungarian rulers of the Austro-Hungarian Empire were greatly resented by the non-Hungarian populations they governed, while the Austrians were regarded as much less oppressive. Western powers viewed Hungary suspiciously as a land filled with landed magnates, an oppressed peasantry, and the Asiatic origins of the Magyars caused further distress.[63] This can be seen in descriptions of Hungarians at the time, such as geographer Leon Dominian's comment that Hungarians were unable to be Germanized due to "the oriental origin of the race."[64] These biases against the Hungarians created a context that would make a fair settlement for Hungary practically impossible.

Hungary was further handicapped by the existence of several secret treaties. Romania remained out of the world war in its initial phases, and finally chose to enter upon signing the Treaty of Bucharest with the United Kingdom, France and Russia in 1916. The Treaty of Bucharest promised Romania all of Transylvania in exchange for a declaration of war on Austria-Hungary and Bulgaria. More than any other promise from the Entente, it was the desire to annex Transylvania that drove Romania into the war.[65] Notably absent from the treaty was the United States, which still remained a neutral power in 1916. Just like the notorious

Treaty of London with Italy, the Treaty of Bucharest violated Wilson's first point calling for open covenants of peace. The Romanians, though, stood to gain much by the enforcement of the secret treaties, thus providing Romania with a natural ally in Italy at the conference.[66]

The Kingdom of Hungary as a whole stood as one of Europe's most diverse at the start of the 20th century. It presented major challenges to cartographers of the time, as seven major nationalities resided within Hungarian territory.[67] In 1910, Hungary reported a population of 21 million people, with 50 percent of them ethnic Hungarians, and the other half comprised of Germans, Slovaks, Serbs, Croats, Ruthenians, Jews, and the largest minority, Romanians, making up 16 percent of the population.[68] Geographically, the Kingdom of Hungary resembled a Hungarian nucleus surrounded by a group of subject nations along the periphery.[69] With Hungary's ethnic diversity, it would be difficult to keep the Hungarian state and meet the Wilsonian principle of self-determination at the same time. For many, it meant that Hungary would shed peripheral territories following the defeat of the Austro-Hungarian Empire at war's end.

Older geographic perspective on "natural frontiers" demonstrated Hungary as a perfect candidate to hold most of its historic territory. From a geographic lens, the Hungarian Plain and the surrounding Carpathian Mountain arc consisted of a perfect unified region. The Hungarians made four points to the peace conference on how Hungarian territory should be dealt with: 1) preserve the geographical, economic and historical unity of their lands, 2) division of Hungary would lead to many persons being under alien rule, 3) Hungary would be willing to give equal rights to all their nationalities following the Swiss model if left intact, and 4) plebiscites, if done fairly, should be allowable to confirm Hungarian sovereignty over these lands.[70] However, the Hungarians were ultimately relying on arguments based upon historic borders or natural features, while the subject nationalities presented arguments based on ethno-linguistic claims and national self-determination. Despite their use of some Wilsonian ideas to support the maintenance of a large Hungarian state, the Wilsonian ideal of self-determination meant that the odds were already stacked up strongly against them.

Hungary faced further challenges during the Paris Peace Conference. Revolution gripped Hungary in 1919, raising alarm among world leadership in Paris. Revolutionary leader Bela Kun declared Hungary a Soviet republic, only the second one in Europe following the creation of the

Soviet Union in 1917. With a new Bolshevik government in Budapest, the Romanian government invaded Hungary with the complicity of the Allied governments in March 1919. It took the Romanians a few months to rout the Bela Kun government, but by midsummer the Romanian army had occupied much of central Hungary, well beyond the borders they had originally claimed in the region. This shift in the political calculus damaged any remaining Hungarian claims being presented at the conference.[71] Moreover, the Romanians hoped for even more territory in exchange for their swift action in stopping the spread of Bolshevism.[72] These claims would be strongly asserted and Romania's action would prove influential on settling the final borders of Hungary.

The Inquiry invested a large amount of research on how best to divide Hungary. The compact mass of Hungarians in the Hungarian Plain would form the nucleus of the proposed new Hungarian state. The Black Book called for Hungary to only retain these areas in the lowlands of the Danube:

> It is recommended that the boundaries of Hungary be established ... so as to release to their respective nationals those elements of the population which desire to be freed from Hungarian rule.
>
> The boundaries of the proposed Hungary do not follow historic lines, and the new state would have but half the area and population that Hungary had before the war. Except along the Czecho-Slovak frontier and in Transylvania, no large compact masses of Magyars would be placed under alien political control. Wherever they are placed under other flags it is because of the geographical separation from the central mass of Magyars or to satisfy vital economic needs of neighboring states.
>
> Further reduction of Hungary along the lines of Czech and Rumanain claims seems eminently undesirable. It would be unwise to give Rumania the mouth of the Maros. Likewise undesirable is the existence of a corridor between Czecho-Slovakia and Jugo-Slavia, since the region of the corridor is preeminently Magyar in character.[73]

This proposed reduction would lead to millions of Magyars residing outside Hungary, mainly in Romania and in the Slovak portion of Czechoslovakia (see chapter 4 on Czechoslovakia for a discussion on the demarcation of this border). While this proposal fell far short of the Wilsonian principle of self-determination, it would fulfill a very different goal—dismantling the empires of old in a manner disadvantageous to the old powerful nationalities. However, the Inquiry did oppose some of the more outrageous claims being made by the new states at Paris. The Czechs wanted to control the entire border area between Austria and Hungary as a corridor to Yugoslavia, and a similar proposal by Romania to gain a link to the Czechs was also considered too much for the American plan.

Despite opposition to some of these claims, large portions of historic Hungary would find their way into Romania, Czechoslovakia and Yugoslavia. The Inquiry proposed two large additions to Romania including all of Transylvania and parts of the Banat (see Figure 3.6):

> It is recommended that all of Transylvania be added to the Rumanian state.
>
> The union of the Rumanians of Transylvania with the Rumanian state is desirable in order that they should be freed from Hungary, by whom they have been harshly treated in the past, and in order that people of like sympathies and speech should be segregated within a common frontier.

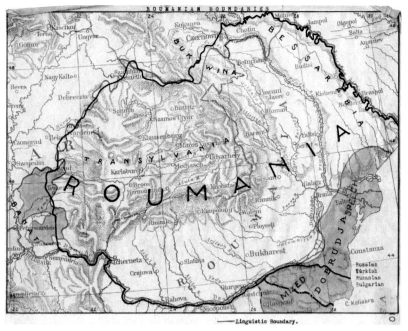

Figure 3.6. *Black Book Map of Romania: The Black Book called for the inclusion of all of Transylvania and the eastern part of the Banat in Romania. The western half of the Banat was to be transferred to Yugoslavia. (Map from JHU Bowman Papers MS 58 13.13)*

If this recommendation is carried out provision should be made for the minority rights of the people in the Magyar (Szekler) area of eastern Transylvania....

It is recommended that the ethnic Rumanian zone in Hungary proper be added to the Rumanian state....

It is recommended that about two-thirds of the Banat be added to the Rumanian state.

In the Banat there is an intermixture of Serbs, Rumanians, and Germans. Of the three counties composing the region, two, Krasso and Temes, are chiefly Rumanain, while the third, Torontal, is predominantly Serb. It is recommended that the two former be assigned to Rumania, that the latter be assigned to Jugo-Slavia, and that the line of division follow the administrative boundaries, because the Hungarian counties are essentially historic entities, corresponding roughly to the Swiss cantons. The utilization of these long-established limits in the running of a new frontier would prevent local administrative confusion.[74]

The Inquiry clearly sided against Hungary's claims by recommending such a large scale transfer of territory. However, compared with the claims forwarded by the other states and with the final borders, as drawn at Paris, the American plan was actually quite lenient.

The settlements with Romania were especially heated and complex. The region of Transylvania held great importance to both peoples. There was, and indeed still is, a very large Hungarian population in Transylvania. This population centered around the city of Koloszvar (today known as Cluj-Napoca in Romania). The mythical founder of Hungary, King Matyas, supposedly came from Koloszvar and the landscape there is replete with institutions that are key to Hungarian national identity.[75] Only Budapest served as a more important center of Hungarian public life than Koloszvar prior to the war. Further to the east of Transylvania's main cities, a second major group of Hungarian speakers were also resident. This group, known as the Szeklers, Hungarian for frontier guardsmen, lived along the eastern edge of the Transylvanian branch of the Carpathian Mountains.

The other major Transylvanian population, the Romanians, also had strong historic ties to Transylvania. The Romanian people long viewed Transylvania as an important part of their nation's territory. Transylvania was viewed as the safe place where Romanians were able to retreat and to save their culture from the onslaught of Slavic peoples and the Turks. The Romanians viewed Transylvania as the "heart" of Romania, and the Hungarian capture of this territory long ago led to the stunting of Romanian development and to the creation of two Romanian states, Wallachia and Moldavia, rather than one greater Romania.[76] This strong identification of Transylvania for the Romanians made the regaining of this land exceptionally important to the young Romanian state. As the Romanians did not have a historic kingdom with which to define their state, they instead chose to include the long-politically separated areas of Transylvania, Wallachia and Moldavia in their definition of the state.[77]

The settlement patterns of the different ethnic groups in both Transylvania and the Banat demonstrated a marked difference. The German and Hungarian populations focused on towns, with the Romanians and Serbs primarily rural and agrarian. This split led to the Hungarian and German populations viewing these populations as simple peasants with low levels of civilization.[78] In many areas, these groups lived in close proximity, often fewer than five miles apart. Since the Hungarian populations were mainly urban, the overall appearance was that of "Hungarian islands" superimposed on a rural Romanian population. Such a settlement pattern made the drawing of an ethno-linguistic border almost impossible. As such, the best solution from the standpoint of self-determination was probably to create Transylvania as an independent multiethnic state, rather than placing such a mixed territory into one nation-state or another.[79]

The Inquiry believed that Hungary's new frontiers should not be based on historic lines, although they conceded that their newly proposed Hungarian state would lose two compact masses of Hungarian population, one to Czechoslovakia and the other to Romania.[80] In the case of Transylvania, experts played down the loss of Hungarian areas, stating that they were sparsely inhabited and therefore of less importance than the size of their areas suggests.[81] The long distance between the Szekler area and the rest of Hungary made it impossible to suggest their remaining in Hungary in any final settlement.[82]

Dividing the Banat would prove much easier (see Figure 3.7). The region had an area where three groups, Hungarians, Romanians and Serbs all lived, but the divisions were clear enough to separate the Romanians and Serbs from each other. The division was successful

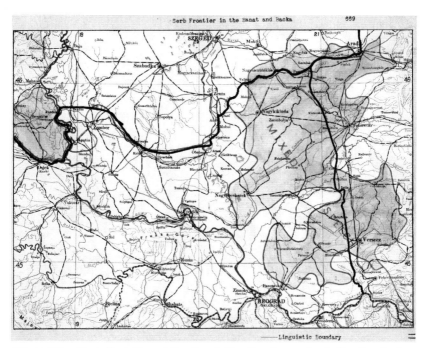

Figure 3.7. *Black Book Map of the Banat: The Banat, a region in the Danube low-lands located at the intersection of Romania, Serbia and Hungary contained mixed populations, as noted by the shaded regions where many ethnic groups shared territory. Hungary retained the northern portion, while Yugoslavia and Romania divided the rest. Yugoslavia would end up with most of the ethnically mixed area, a region today known as Vojvodina, which is one of the most ethnically mixed areas in modern Serbia. (Map from JHU Bowman Papers MS 58 13.13)*

enough that only about 7,500 Romanians were left in Yugoslavia and only about 6,500 Serbs in Romania.[83] As in other similar cases, it was the losing power, Hungary, that faced the total loss of their populace in much of the region. Hungary did maintain the northernmost portions of the Banat where the population was almost all Hungarian, but the mixed areas were mostly transferred to Yugoslavia and Romania.

During the peace conference, the Coolidge Mission visited Hungary and Romania, providing more evidence to support the dramatic reduction of Hungary, especially in its border with Romania. The Coolidge reports clearly outlined the full justifications both Hungary and Romania made to substantiate their claims to Transylvania. Romania cited: a population majority; control of the majority of the area; the oppression of Romanian majority under the old Hungarian kingdom; Transylvania would vindicate the Romanian historical claims to the area; and, the Allies had promised them the territory in the Treaty of Bucharest.[84] Hungary claimed: the superiority of Hungarian over Romanian "Kultur"; the long-standing economic affiliation of Transylvania with Hungary; the inefficiency of the Romanian government; the continuity of their historic territory; and, transfer of Transylvania to Romania threatened to cause a disruption to the peace of Europe.[85] The Romanians had mastered the rhetoric of Wilson while the Hungarians seemed to be relying on both threats and pre-Wilsonian power-based diplomacy to substantiate their claims. The Hungarians even threatened that if Hungary were dismantled they would never cease to "agitate and to be a source of irritation for their neighbors."[86]

Along with sending Professor Coolidge, the Big Four states created the "Committee for the Study of Territorial Questions Relating to Rumania and Yugoslavia" prior to their discussions as to how these states' new borders should be shaped, so that a full study of the ethnic complexities of the Balkans would be on record for the plenipotentiaries to base their decisions upon. The Committee included two American Inquiry members considered to be experts on Austria-Hungary, Drs. Clive Day and Charles Seymour.[87] Although only the Big Four had representation on the Committee, Romanian Prime Minister Bratianu was among those called before the group to speak. As a defeated power, the Hungarian side was not given an opportunity to address the Committee.

On April 6, 1919, the Committee published its report on Romania, which included several recommendations pertaining to Transylvania. Principles were delineated in the final demarcation of a border between Hungary and Romania. The Committee stated that the ethnic principle could not always be followed along the linguistic frontier due to its complexity; therefore, weight should be given toward the Romanian side in areas where Hungarian towns are surrounded by a Romanian-inhabited countryside.[88] The Committee also called for the final treaty to guarantee complete autonomy to all minority groups in Transylvania regarding local administration, education and religion. The final border proposed by the Committee was less than that called for by Romania, but included more territory than that of the Inquiry line initially proposed by the United States (see Figure 3.8). The Committee-proposed border assigned 4.3 million people from Transylvania and neighboring

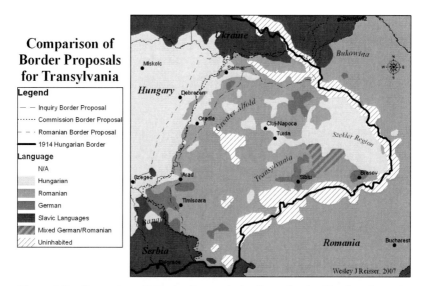

Comparison of Border Proposals for Transylvania

Legend

— — Inquiry Border Proposal
······· Commission Border Proposal
— · · Romanian Border Proposal
——— 1914 Hungarian Border

Language
    N/A
    Hungarian
    Romanian
    German
    Slavic Languages
    Mixed German/Romanian
    Uninhabited

Wesley J Reisser, 2007

Figure 3.8. *Comparison of Border Proposals for Transylvania: The American plan provided for a border east of both the Romanian claim and the border agreed to at the peace conference. The border proposed by the Committee at the peace conference was eventually adopted for use in the Treaty of Trianon and remains the border between Hungary and Romania today. (Cartography by the author)*

areas, including 2.3 million Romanians and 1.9 million others, to Romania.[89] This countermanded the Romanian proposed line that would have netted them 4.9 million people, including 2.6 million persons not of Romanian nationality.[90] Although the Committee report ameliorated somewhat the Romanian claim, this solution still left a huge minority problem within the proposed border.

Despite the Romanian intervention in Hungary, as the treaty moved forward the Committee-proposed line remained the basis for the final settlement. The Bela Kun government was replaced with a conservative government in Budapest, which was then presented with the Treaty of Trianon in January 1920. The final treaty removed huge segments of Hungarian territory, and was only ratified under intense pressure that November. Hungary lost over two-thirds of its land and people in the Treaty of Trianon, and went on to be a very disruptive element in Central Europe during the interwar period.[91] In the end, Hungary retained only 36,000 square miles of the original Kingdom of Hungary's 126,000 square miles of territory, with Romania being the largest beneficiary, receiving 40,000 square miles of territory.[92] These new borders ran through areas of mixed nationality. Besides the dramatic loss of land, Trianon left Hungary with only three-fifths of its prewar population, including the loss of three million Hungarians into neighboring countries.[93] This was a staggering political and economic loss for the Hungarians.

The final Treaty of Trianon gave the benefit of the doubt to any party other than Hungary. This perception, along with the fact that Hungary was not given a chance to present its case to the peace conference, gave rise to a perception among all in Hungary that the terms were imposed upon them. This substantiates claims made that the victors were given too much license in the production of new borders. The Treaty of Trianon ended up being the most severe of the World War I peace treaties, much more so than Versailles.[94] American geographer, Isaiah Bowman, summarized the Hungarian situation as, "It was the fate of Hungary to be caught between the effects of defeat on the one hand and of claims of oppression on the other and to suffer the consequences."[95]

In the immediate postwar period, it seemed obvious that Hungary would try to regain lost territories. How they would go about this was less evident at the time. During World War II, the Hungarian government aligned with Adolf Hitler, partly due to promises of regaining Transylvania.[96] Through the "Vienna Awards," Hitler allotted the northern two-thirds of Transylvania to Hungary, including the Szekler area, while maintaining the southern sections of Transylvania inside Nazi-occupied Romania. Due to this change in territory, the Romanians allied with the Soviet Red Army to regain northern Transylvania from Hungary.[97] At the end of the Second World War, the borders of Hungary were restored to the Treaty of Trianon delimited frontiers and they have remained as such.

FINLAND, ESTONIA & LATVIA

Prior to the war, Finland and the three Baltic states—Estonia, Latvia and Lithuania (see chapter 4 for Lithuania)—had been a part of Tsarist Russia. Russia had entered the war in 1914 as one of the key members of the Entente. However, with the dissolution of the Romanov dynasty and the ensuing Russian Revolution of 1917, many western and southern peripheral regions of the Empire were suddenly in a position to secede from Russia. A series of national committees emerged and quickly declared independence from the collapsing Russian Empire. Russia was the world's largest territorial state and home to enormous minority populations, thus making it a target for dismantlement based on Wilsonian principles. Because of the tumult in Russia and a lack of any representation at the Paris Peace Conference, the drawing of these borders went forward with very little controversy between the Big Four. Discussions of Russia were constant, but they usually were cursory because of the fluid situation.[98]

During the research phase of the Inquiry, and indeed throughout the entire Paris Peace Conference, the status of Russia remained in question. As the revolution raged, it was unclear whether the communist Reds or nationalist Whites would emerge victorious. Thus, plans moved forward within the Inquiry as to how to handle the regions of Russia and in how they should be disposed of following the war, in a manner that all but ignored the events in central Russia itself. Finland, Estonia and Latvia would emerge from the Paris Peace Conference with borders quite similar to those they control today, while other parts of the Russian Empire would fare quite differently (see chapter 5 for discussions on Ukraine, the Caucuses and Central Asia).

Finland maintained the strongest position of any of these breakaway regions of Russia, as Finland held a special status within the Russian Empire. The Grand Duchy of Finland only became part of Russia in 1809 following the Russo-Swedish War. It had functioned as a semi-autonomous region within the Russian Empire and declared independence from Russia on December 6, 1917, just months into the Russian Revolution.

Sentiments toward Finland ran strong among the American experts. In the final years of the Russian Empire, Finland had lost its autonomous status and a process of Slavicization was imposed upon the territory.[99] Other than within the Aaland Islands and directly along the Swedish border, Finland contained a compact mass of Finnish speakers, a truly distinct group by virtue of their non-Indo-European language. The Inquiry recommended that Finland gain full independence from Russia as part of the peace settlement (see Figure 3.9):

[I]t may be noted that they [Finland, along with several areas to be discussed in chapter 7] represent nationalities whose severance from the Russian Empire would not destroy the Russian economic fabric, and would at the same time liberate peoples who, because of historic oppressions and geographical position, would probably develop a stronger political and economic life if permitted to separate from the rest of the former Russian Empire.[100]

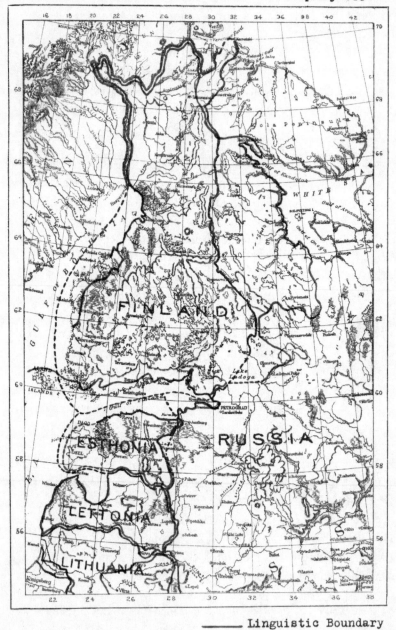

_____ Linguistic Boundary

Figure 3.9. *Black Book Map of Finland and the Baltic States: The Inquiry proposed the creation of separate states for the Finns and each of the three Baltic peoples. Other than Lithuania, these states emerged from the Paris Peace Conference with borders quite similar to those in place today. (Map from JHU Bowman Papers MS 58 13.13)*

The Black Book also called for the transfer of the Aaland Islands from Russia to Sweden because of their Swedish population. Because of Sweden's neutrality in the war, no adjustment in the Finnish border with Sweden was called for other than the return of the Aaland Islands, located in the Gulf of Bothnia between Finland and Sweden, which had been Swedish territory prior to the Russo-Swedish War of 1808.

At the conference, high level discussions on Finland began in April, with Wilson looking far more favorably on recognition of Finland than either Lloyd George or Clemenceau.[101] However, the Finns themselves laid claim to vast areas beyond what the United States had proposed for the Finnish state, including Karelia and the Kola Peninsula—large areas east of Finnish territory, along with territory on the Gulf of Finland that was very close to Petrograd (modern St. Petersburg).[102] These areas were not considered by the Big Four and once a commission was set up to explore Finland's borders, it was determined that the borders should remain similar to those in the initial American proposal. Finally, on May 26, the Big Four wrote to Admiral Koltchak, the leader of the White armies in Russia, and in that letter recognized that the Allies were extending formal recognition to Finland as an independent state.[103] Rather than specifying the border, they deferred to the League of Nations any final determination on the Russo-Finnish boundary. With the continued tumult in Russia, the border ended up being demarcated and agreed upon between Russia and Finland after the Russian Revolution ended. The 1920 agreement kept Karelia as part of Russia, but granted it autonomy (a status still technically enjoyed by the region today).[104]

The Inquiry did call for the transfer of the Aaland Islands to Sweden, although they were under Finnish control at the time of the peace conference. Rather than being addressed directly at the conference, the final disposition of the islands was given to the League of Nations, which in 1922 ordered that Finland would remain in control, as long as the local population of Swedish speakers were granted a degree of autonomy.[105]

Finland's borders, as set after World War I, remain in place today with one major exception. Finland lost part of its southeastern corner, around Lake Ladoga, to the Soviet Union following the Winter War, a conflict in the first year of the Second World War, between Finland and the USSR. However, the principal legacy of the conference regarding the creation of Finland remains in place today, as this small state remains independent along lines similar to those proposed and championed by the American delegation to Paris.

The Baltic States would prove far more difficult for the conference than Finland, mainly due to their small size, tiny populations, and tenuous position. Following the Treaty of Brest-Litovsk, which ended the German-Russian component of World War I, the Germans had taken control of the Baltic region from Russia. The presence of Russian and German populations mixed in with the Baltic peoples further complicated the situation. German Freikorps had seized control of large areas and were terrorizing the local populations. The national committees in both Estonia and Latvia went forward with efforts at independence, despite the incredible instability in the area. Estonia declared independence on February 23, 1918, and Latvia on November 18 of the same year.

Unlike Finland, the Inquiry's initial recommendation for the newly declared Baltic States was less clear-cut in favor of their independence. These states were each very small in both area and population, hardly in a strong and defensible position next door to the largest state on the globe, and one that had ruled over these territories for hundreds of years. Rather than recommending total independence, the Inquiry proposed that they hold referendums on rejoining a federalized or democratic Russian state. They clearly recognized that such a course of action could only take place if the Bolsheviks lost the Russian Civil War. Otherwise, there was no willingness to place these territories inside a communist state. The Black Book proposed:

> It is recommended that encouragement be given, at opportune times, to the reunion with Russia of those border regions of the south and west which have broken away and set up their own national governments, particularly the Baltic Provinces and the Ukraine, if reunion can be accomplished within a federalized or genuinely democratic Russia.
>
> Russia may be divided into great natural regions, each with its own distinctive economic life. No one region is self-sufficient enough to form a strong state. The economic welfare of all would be served by reunion on a federal basis, which would, of course, also have other evident advantages.
>
> On the other hand, if the Bolshevist government is in power and is continuing its present course at the time when Russian territorial questions are settled at the peace conference, there seems to be no alternative to accepting the independence and tracing the frontiers of all the non-Russian nationalities under discussion.

It may, however, be advisable to make recognition of such countries as the Ukraine or the Esth or Lettish republics conditional upon the holding of a referendum some years later upon the question of reunion with Russia.[106]

Clearly, with the victory of the Bolsheviks, no such referendums would ever come about.

Specifically for Estonia, the Black Book called for a new state along the following lines:

> The limits of the proposed state practically coincide with the limits of the Esth ethnic area, and on the east with the administrative frontier of the Baltic Provinces and Russia proper. Only on the southeast does it encroach on historically Russian territory to take in the Pechory district, inhabited primarily by Esths.[107]

Latvia, then known by the Americans as Lettonia, was also proposed in the Black Book:

> The proposed state of Lettonia is limited by boundaries which follow remarkably clean-cut and long-standing Lettish ethnic frontiers, and cannot be defined in terms of natural features because there is a striking absence of topographic relief. As drawn upon the map the line corresponds nearly everywhere to the boundaries of existing administrative divisions.[108]

At the conference, the Commission on Baltic Affairs was set up to consider the Baltic States. In its reports to the Big Four, the Commission hewed closely with the American position on the demarcation of Estonia and Latvia. Neither state was directly created at the conference though, as their territories were entirely carved out of Russia and no treaty with Russia was concluded. Both states received full western recognition in 1921, following 1920 treaties with the Soviet Union that acknowledged their American-proposed borders and their full independence.

During World War II, both Estonia and Latvia were absorbed into the Soviet Union during the Red Army's western march that followed the Nazi invasion. However, the United States and many other western states refused to recognize the Soviet annexation of these countries. In 1990, the Baltic States were the first republics to declare independence from the USSR and both Estonia and Latvia reemerged onto the world stage with their post–World War I boundaries.

SHRINKING BULGARIA

Bulgaria, the sole Balkan state to side with the Central Powers, found it-self victim of the carving knife, as did the other losing powers at the Paris Peace Conference. Prior to the outbreak of World War I in the western Balkans, Bulgaria had been involved in the two Balkan Wars, the second of which ended only one year before World War I erupted. In the Second Balkan War, Bulgaria lost most of the territories it had gained in the First Balkan War, a couple years prior, and was thus easily lured by Austria-Hungary to fight against Serbia to regain these lands, most of which now lie within the Republic of Macedonia. Despite being one of the Central Powers, Bulgaria came closer than any other to making territorial gains, mainly because the United States remained friendly toward Bulgaria (the United States never declared war on either Bulgaria or the Ottoman Em-pire) and because Bulgaria's enemies were more focused elsewhere.[109]

In one region, the Dobrudja, located along the lower reaches of the Danube River and into the Danube delta, Bulgaria would find itself in a position where the United States advocated for a territorial transfer from Allied Romania to an enemy state. Bulgaria had military control of the area at the time, but nonetheless, this was highly unusual at a conference where the non-American delegations were busy engaging in a "to the victor go the spoils" method of territorial disposition. The Inquiry proposed dividing the Dobrudja by returning some areas to Bulgaria (see Figure 3.10):

> It is recommended that in the case of the Dobrudja the Rumanian-Bulgarian frontier which existed before 1913 be restored, with slight modifications...
>
> Moreover, to place the boundary farther south, to meet Rumania's desire for better harbor facilities, would violate the principle of self-determination and hurt Bulgaria far more seriously that it would help Rumania.
>
> Rumania could not well object, in view of her very generous gains elsewhere.[110]

Clearly, the Inquiry applied Wilsonian principles to the northern border of Bulgaria. Demography clearly favored the Bulgarians, as the region contained almost 300,000 people, of whom all but around 10,000 were Bulgarian.[111] However, the other states at Paris were unwilling to even

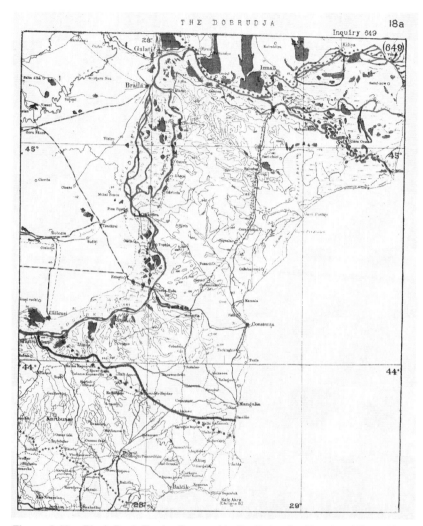

Figure 3.10. *Black Book Border Proposal in the Dobrudja: Despite siding with the Central Powers, there was strong American support for Bulgaria receiving the southern portion of the Dobrudja. The Black Book map proposed a border based on the ethno-linguistic frontier (dark line in the map), in place of the more southerly border seen near the bottom of the map as a dotted line. (Map from JHU Bowman Papers MS 58 13.13)*

consider such a transfer. Throughout the summer of 1919, the American delegation pushed strongly for the Bulgarians to regain the portions of the Dobrudja lost in 1913, but to no avail. The initial report of the Romanian Committee proposed the possibility of a small concession by Romania of ethnic Bulgarian areas, but more generally it concluded that it was beyond its purview to "recommend a modification of the frontier which would involve the cession to an enemy State of a territory forming *de facto and de jure* an integral part of an Allied State."[112] The Dobrudja region remained in Romanian hands until World War II, when the border adjusted back slightly in favor of Bulgaria. This is the only portion of Bulgaria's borders that changed since the World War I era.

The American plan was not adopted for the northern border, and to the south and west Bulgaria would also receive borders quite different than those envisioned by the Inquiry. It lost access to the Aegean Sea to the south with Greece's extension of territory through southern Thrace to the Turkish border. This particular extension of territory was not without controversy, as the American proposal advocated for Bulgaria keeping this region:

> The coastal belt assigned to Bulgaria by the treaty which closed the Second Balkan War is much less than that desired by Bulgaria, and deprives her of the harbor of Kavala which she claims as an essential outlet for her western commerce. It is recommended that the coastal belt be maintained as in 1914 in order to prevent the roundabout routing of Bulgaria's trade by way of the Black Sea and the Bosphorus.
>
> The Greeks lay claim to the whole littoral to the east of Kavala through Thrace to the shores of the Black Sea. True, they formed the largest element of the population next to the Turks, but to grant them this strip would bar the direct access of Bulgaria to the sea, and would engender great bitterness that might even lead to war.[113]

Greece wanted control of Western Thrace, a region Bulgaria had acquired in the Balkan Wars. Along the coast, there were large Greek populations, but the overall population was mixed among Greeks, Bulgarians and Turks.[114] Greece also wanted control of Eastern Thrace, including portions that would remain in Bulgaria and Turkey. They would only gain the western portion, which has remained Greek territory ever since. The impact on Bulgaria was significant, as the state lost its access to the Aegean Sea and has only been able to access the high seas via the Bosporus Straits ever since.

Bulgaria also lost a small area along the border with Yugoslavia. Four areas, the Timok valley, Tsaribrod, Strumitsa and Bosilegrad were ceded to Yugoslavia to protect Serb railway routes from Bulgarian attack. All three areas were largely ethnically Bulgarian and should have been kept in that state based on the principle of self-determination.[115] Bulgaria lost about 48,000 people to Yugoslavia in these transfers.

The American plan for peace not only called for less territorial reduction to Bulgaria than was carried out, but actually called for an extension of Bulgarian territory to the southeast, in line with the creation of a new straits zone around the Bosporus (see chapter 5). This, along with the American proposal to extend Bulgarian control in the southern Dobrudja, to hold the border with Yugoslavia along the already demarcated Serb-Bulgarian boundary, and to keep Western Thrace in Bulgaria shows that American influence over many of the territorial decisions made at Paris were minimal—especially the further south and east one went on the map of Europe. A combination of factors made the American program untenable regarding Bulgaria, including the United States' lack of a state of war with Bulgaria and a general conviction in Paris that the Central Powers would all suffer territorial loss as punishment for their involvement in the war. Other than the minor adjustment to the Dobrudja made in 1945, Bulgaria holds these World War I–era borders today.

The long-lasting nature of so many border proposals made at Paris reveals just how relevant the Paris Peace Conference remains today. These borders have indeed shown tremendous staying power over a turbulent period in world history. Of course many of these borders remained controversial long after the war, leading to widespread revisionist thinking among the peoples and states that lost territory at the peace conference.

NOTES

1. Address of President Wilson to Congress, January 8, 1918. In Arthur Link. *The Papers of Woodrow Wilson, Volume 45*. Princeton: Princeton University Press, 1984. Pg. 536.

2. Charles Haskins. 1921. "The New Boundaries of Germany," in *What Really Happened at Paris: The Story of the Peace Conference, 1918–1919 by American Delegates*, ed. Edward House. New York: Charles Scribner's Sons.

3. Isaiah Bowman. 1928. *The New World: Problems in Political Geography*. New York: World Book. Pg. 194.

4. Harold Callender. 1927. "Alsace-Lorraine Since the War." *Foreign Affairs* (5:3). Pg. 430.

5. Bowman, 1928. Pg. 201–202.

6. Treaty of Versailles, Articles 50–79.

7. Draft Reply of the Commission on Belgian and Danish Affairs to the Remarks of the German Delegation on the Conditions of Peace: FRUS Vol. VI. Pg. 464.

8. Treaty of Versailles, Article 34.

9. Robert George. 1927. "Eupen and Malmedy." *Foreign Affairs* (5:2).

10. Haskins, 1921. Pg. 54.

11. Black Book. Pg. 8.

12. Margaret MacMillan. 2001. *Paris 1919*. New York: Random House. Pg. 170.

13. Notes of a Meeting Held in Mr. Lloyd George's Residence at 23, Rue Nitot on Tuesday, April 8, at 11 a.m.: FRUS Vol. V. Pg. 66.

14. Treaty of Versailles, Articles 34–40.

15. Colbert Held. 1951. "The New Saarland." *Geographical Review* (41:4). Pg. 597.

16. Bowman, 1928. Pg. 268.

17. Haskins, 1921. Pg. 42.

18. Black Book. Pg. 13.

19. Ibid.

20. The Secretary of State to the Special Representative (House), 11/21/1918: FRUS Vol. II. Pg. 450.

21. MacMillan, 2001. Pg. 169–170.

22. J.A. Laponce. 2004. "Turning Votes into Territories: Boundary Referendum's in Theory and Practice." *Political Geography* (23:2).

23. Leon Dominian. 1917. *Frontiers of Language and Nationality in Europe*. New York: Henry Hold and Company.

24. Ibid.

25. Leon Dominian. 1918. "The Nationality Map of Europe," in *League of Nations*. Boston: World Peace Foundation.

26. Bowman, 1928.

27. George White. 2000. *Nationalism and Territory: Constructing Group Identity in Southeastern Europe*. Lanham, MD: Rowman & Littlefield Publishers.

28. Paul Mowrer. 1921. *Balkanized Europe: A Study in Political Analysis and Reconstruction*. New York: E.P. Dutton & Co. Pg. 172.

29. Address of President Wilson to Congress, January 8, 1918. In Arthur Link. 1984. *The Papers of Woodrow Wilson, Volume 45*. Princeton: Princeton University Press. Pg. 536.

30. Text of the President's Note to Austria-Hungary of 10/18/1918, as published in the *New York Times* 10/20/1918.

31. Black Book. Pg. 52.

32. Black Book. Pg. 53.

33. Charles Seymour. 1921. "The End of an Empire: Remnants of Austria-Hungary," in *What Really Happened at Paris: The Story of the Peace Conference, 1918–1919 by American Delegates*, ed. Edward House. New York: Charles Scribner's Sons. Pg. 95.

34. MacMillan, 2001. Pg. 246.

35. Professor A.C. Coolidge to the Commission to Negotiate Peace, Berne, 12/31/1918: FRUS Vol. II. Pg. 220.

36. Notes of a Meeting Held at the Quai d'Orsay, Paris, on Friday, May 2, 1919, at 4 p.m.: FRUS Vol. V. Pg. 425.

37. Douglas Johnson. 1917. "The Role of Political Boundaries." *Geographical Review* (4:3).

38. Ibid.

39. Bowman, 1928.

40. Johnson, 1917.

41. Link, 1984. Pg. 536.

42. Address of President Wilson to Congress, January 8, 1918.

43. Richard Hartshorne. 1938. "A Survey of the Boundary Problems of Europe," in Charles Colby, *Geographic Aspects of International Relations*. Chicago: University of Chicago.

44. Dominian, 1917.

45. Guido Weigend. 1950. "Effects of Boundary Changes in the South Tyrol." *Geographical Review* (40:3).

46. Black Book. Pg. 48–49.

47. Black Book, Pg. 47: JHU Bowman Papers Box 13.13.

48. Ibid.

49. Ibid.

50. Ibid.

51. Black Book, Pg. 48: JHU Bowman Papers Box 13.13.

52. Ibid.

53. Professor A.C. Coolidge to the Commission to Negotiate Peace: FRUS Vol. II, Pg. 226.

54. Memorandum by Professor A.C. Coolidge: FRUS Vol. XII, Pg. 277.

55. Professor A.C. Coolidge to the Commission to Negotiate Peace: FRUS Vol. XII, Pgs. 282–284.

56. Notes of a Meeting of the Big Four 4/19/1919: FRUS Vol. V, Pgs. 80–94.

57. President Wilson's manifesto of April 23, 1919, in Ray Baker. 1922. *Woodrow Wilson and World Settlement Vol. III*. Garden City, NY: Doubleday Page. Pg. 287.

58. David Stevenson. 2004. *Cataclysm: The First World War as Political Tragedy*. New York: Basic Books.

59. Professor A.C. Coolidge to the Commission to Negotiate Peace: FRUS Vol. XII, Pg. 307.

60. Notes from The Council of Foreign Ministers 5/10/1919: FRUS Vol. IV, Pg. 699.

61. Douglas Johnson, 1921. "Fiume and the Adriatic Problem," in *What Really Happened at Paris: The Story of the Peace Conference, 1918–1919 by American Delegates*, ed. Edward House. New York: Charles Scribner's Sons. Pg. 126.

62. Isaiah Bowman to Eduard Bruckner, February 25, 1920 (Collection of the American Geographical Society) in Martin, Geoffrey. 1980. *The Life and Thought of Isaiah Bowman*. Hamden, Archon Books. Pg. 97.

63. MacMillan, 2001. Pg. 257.

64. Dominian, 1917. Pg. 154.

65. Stevenson, 2004; White, 2000.

66. David Andelman. 2008. *A Shattered Peace: Versailles 1919 and the Price We Pay Today*. Hoboken, NJ: John Wiley & Sons. Pg. 230.

67. B.C. Wallis. 1916. "Distribution of Nationalities in Hungary." *The Geographical Journal* (47:3).

68. B.C. Wallis. 1918 (ii). "The Rumanians in Hungary." *Geographical Review* (6:2).

69. B.C. Wallis. 1921. "The Dismemberment of Hungary." *Geographical Review* (11:3).

70. Mowrer, 1921.

71. Bowman, 1928; Stevenson, 2004; White, 2000.

72. Bowman, 1928.

73. Black Book. Pg. 55.

74. Black Book Pg. 36–37.

75. White, 2000.

76. Ibid.

77. Ibid.

78. Ibid.

79. Hugh Seton-Watson. 1977. *Nations and States: An Enquiry into the Origins of Nations and the Politics of Nationalism*. Boulder, CO: Westview Press. Pg. 183.

80. Wallis, 1916.

81. Wallis, 1918 (ii).

82. Bowman, 1928.

83. Andelman, 2008. Pg. 237.

84. Captain Nicholas Roosevelt to Professor A.C. Coolidge: FRUS Vol. XII, Pg. 407–410.

85. Ibid.

86. Ibid.

87. Committee for the Study of Territorial Questions Relating to Rumania and Yugoslavia. *Report No. 1: Rumanian Frontiers*. Paris: April 6, 1919. Pg. 3.

88. Committee for the Study of Territorial Questions Relating to Rumania and Yugoslavia, 1919. Pgs. 6–7.

89. Committee for the Study of Territorial Questions Relating to Rumania and Yugoslavia, 1919. Pg. 17.

90. Ibid.

91. Bowman, 1928.

92. Wallis, 1921.

93. Rogers Brubaker. 1997."Aftermaths of Empire and the Unmixing of Peoples," in Karen Barkey and Mark von Hagen, *After Empire: Multi-Ethnic Societies and Nation-Building*. Boulder, CO: Westview Press; Bowman, 1928.

94. White, 2000.

95. Bowman, 1928. Pg. 322.

96. John Cadzow. 1983. *Transylvania: The Roots of Ethnic Conflict*. Kent, Ohio: Kent State Press.

97. White, 2000.

98. MacMillan, 2001. Pg. 65.

99. Leon Dominian. 1915. "Linguistic Areas in Europe: Their Boundaries and Political Significance." *Bulletin of the American Geographical Society* (47:6). Pg. 420.

100. Black Book. Pg. 17.

101. Notes of a Meeting Held at President Wilson's Residence in the Place des Etats-Unis, Paris, on Monday, April 28, 1919, at 11 a.m.: FRUS Vol. V. Pg. 316.

102. Notes of a Meeting Held at President Wilson's Residence in the Place des Etats-Unis, Paris, on Saturday, May 10, 1919, at 12 noon: FRUS Vol. V. Pg. 551.

103. Despatch to Admiral Koltchak: FRUS Vol. VI. Pg. 36.

104. Bowman, 1928. Pg. 448.

105. Bowman, 1928. Pg. 447.

106. Black Book. Pg. 16.

107. Black Book. Pg. 20.

108. Black Book. Pg. 20.

109. MacMillan, 2001. Pg. 136.

110. Black Book. Pg. 37–39.

111. MacMillan, 2001. Pg. 140.

112. Committee for the Study of Territorial Questions Related to Rumania and Yugoslavia, Report No. 1. 1919.

113. Black Book. Pg. 62.

114. Bowman, 1928. Pg. 401–402.

115. Isaiah Bowman. 1921. "Constantinople and the Balkans," in *What Really Happened at Paris: The Story of the Peace Conference, 1918–1919 by American Delegates*, ed. Edward House. New York: Charles Scribner's Sons. Pg. 166.

CHAPTER 4

Negotiating Borders Part 2— A Survey of Boundaries Drawn in 1919 That Have Disappeared

The Paris Peace Conference witnessed the birth of a series of states and new borders that would face tremendous turmoil and shifts in the decades following their creation. Some of these states, namely Czechoslovakia and Yugoslavia, would persist for only a matter of decades before they also disintegrated, much like the empires they emerged out of in 1919. Despite this, the legacy of the creation of these, and of new states that did survive—although with different boundaries—remains significant to this day. Many of the great challenges in the history of Europe in the later 20th century can be traced to a series of decisions from the conference that have since been overturned. In some of these cases, the position of the United States has been vindicated, while in many others the proposals it forwarded were adopted and since overturned.

POLAND AND THE CORRIDOR

The rebirth of Poland was one of President Wilson's principal goals going into the Paris Peace Conference. Prior to the three partitions of Poland in 1772, 1793, and 1795, Poland was one of Europe's largest territorial states. After the partitions, Prussia, Austria and Russia had completely devoured Poland, leaving sizeable Polish populations in all three empires. A new, large Polish state would indeed emerge from Paris, but along boundaries dramatically different from those of either historic Poland or the modern Polish state.

The re-creation of Poland was foreseen as one of the United States major goals when it entered the First World War. The newly reborn state was promised unfettered access to the sea in the thirteenth of Wilson's Fourteen Points:

> XIII. An independent Polish state should be erected which should include the territories inhabited by indisputably Polish populations, which should be assured a free and secure access to the sea, and whose political and economic independence and territorial integrity should be guaranteed by international covenant.[1]

Although many of the Fourteen Points were not accepted by the other Great Powers, in the case of Poland, this point served as the principal reference at the conference for the work of the Polish Commission and would be fulfilled, as outlined, in the final treaties.[2] Both Britain and France joined the United States as enthusiastic supporters of the Polish cause.

Polish claims, as presented both before and during the conference, centered on the re-creation of the historic medieval Polish kingdom. However, historic Poland incorporated a much larger state than the area in which Polish people constituted the majority.[3] This ran counter to Wilson's view of how Poland should be shaped when it was to be re-born. The President viewed the Polish problem as the lack of self-determination for the Polish people, rather than the lack of the old Polish kingdom, and he thus supported the creation of a Poland only within the regions where there was a Polish majority.[4] Historic Poland, in union with Lithuania, extended into areas with clear Ukrainian, Belarussian, Lithuanian and Russian populations, along with small amounts of many other ethnic groups, not to mention a huge Jewish population concentrated in the cities throughout the entire region.

Prior to the establishment of the Inquiry, American scholars who would later become involved in preparations for peace were already focused on the problem of Poland. Inquiry scholars noted that large Polish populations lived in all three of the states that partitioned it.[5] Russia claimed the largest concentration of Poles, with smaller contingents in the German provinces of Posen and Silesia and in the Austrian province of Galicia. There was tremendous interest in finding a way to create a state for what was probably the largest national group without a state on the European continent.

The Black Book unequivocally calls for the creation of Poland (see Figure 4.1):

Figure 4.1. *Black Book Map of Poland and Lithuania: The Inquiry proposed a Polish state that was much smaller than the one finally created at the Paris Peace Conference. Much of what was allocated to Lithuania by the Inquiry would end up in Poland, along with areas considered for addition to Ukraine that were also taken by Poland after the conference ended. (Map from JHU Bowman Papers MS 58 13.13)*

It is recommended: That a) an independent Polish state be established which b) shall include indisputably Polish populations.

The world has agreed that a Polish state shall be established which shall be politically, and, as far as possible, economically independent.

If a new Polish state is formed it follows that the frontier should be drawn so as to include all of the Polish majorities contiguous to the main group, in order not to leave upon the outside Polish districts that may form the center of irredentist movements.

The eastern frontier assigned on the map to the Polish-Lithuanian-Catholic White Russian complex ought to stand, because it is based primarily on the line of religious division between Catholics and Orthodox.

The proposed Poland might include on the southeast the hotly disputed and very puzzling territory and population of eastern Galicia, included between the solid and the dotted lines on the map. The region should be assigned to Poland only if the Ukraine is in its present state of chaos, and then only as a self-governing province, guaranteed by the League of Nations the right to decide its own allegiance at a later date....

To the west, in Germany, the boundary has been drawn so as to include only unmistakably Polish territory, in so far as the sinuosities of the linguistic frontier permit.[6]

Furthermore, the Black Book called for the creation of the so-called Polish Corridor, a route to the sea for Poland that would create some strife at the conference, but especially cause problems with Germany over the coming decades:

It is recommended that Poland be given a secure and unhampered access to the Baltic. The problem of Polish access to the sea is very difficult. If such access is accorded through continuous Polish territory, the province of East Prussia, with a population of 1,600,000 Germans, will be cut off from the rest of Germany. If Poland does not secure access to the sea, 600,000 Poles in West Prussia will remain under German rule and 20,000,000 Poles in Poland proper will probably have but a hampered and precarious commercial outlet, subject to alien and, for a time at least, hostile... decision.

It is believed that the lesser of these evils is preferable, and that the "Corridor" and Danzig should be ceded to Poland, as shown on map 6. East Prussia, though territorially cut off from the rest of Germany, could easily be assured railroad transit across the Polish corridor (a simple matter as compared with assuring port facilities to Poland), and has, in addition, excellent communication via Königsberg and the Baltic.[7]

The creation of Poland would prove complex. It presented two challenges: 1) how to deal with an eastern border for Poland despite the countries at the peace conference not recognizing the government of the USSR to Poland's east, and 2) how to draw the western border, which would result in a huge loss of German territory. The complexities in creating Poland were so immense that the Commission on Polish Affairs would meet more times than any other at the conference.[8] The Commission included many highly influential advisors to the Big Four delegations. Most notably, the main American representative on the Commission was none other than Isaiah Bowman, chief architect of the Black Book.[9] Bowman came to be associated with the work of the Polish Commission more than almost anyone in Paris. The Commission relied on Bowman's expertise, and even more so, on his maps.

The Inquiry map of Poland and the ethnic maps created for the region were a principal source for the Polish Commission in making its final recommendations.[10]

The Commission on Polish Affairs released its report on borders with Germany in March, after almost two full months of closed deliberations. The report outlines the key considerations that were used to delimit Poland's western border:

a. That primary consideration be given to the line of ethnic separation in such a way as to secure the fairest possible settlement between the two peoples concerned.

b. That rectification of the frontier, in some places in favour of the Poles and others in favour of the Germans, be made where the ethnic facts are outweighed by the other factors and principles involved.[11]

Reliance on ethnic factors alone left one major problem, and that was the promise that Poland be granted access to the sea, as the German population along the entire Baltic Sea coast outnumbered the Polish population. At that point, it was proposed that the city of Danzig (now known as Gdansk) be ceded to Poland, as this was the port best suited for use by Poland along a corridor to the sea. Danzig sat near the mouth of the Vistula River, which serves as the principal waterway through Poland, and also cuts through Warsaw, which was envisioned as the new capital city of the country. It was also the main port along this stretch of the Baltic coast. It therefore seemed a good choice for Poland's main port. As can be seen in the Inquiry map, the Polish Corridor to the sea would cut Germany in two, as the large German population of East Prussia was to be kept in the German state based on the principle of self-determination. The Commission defended its position that the Polish Corridor needed to include Danzig:

The legitimate aspirations of the Polish people for an outlet to the sea, as endorsed by Allied statesmen, cannot be fulfilled unless Dantzig becomes a Polish port....

The so-called Polish corridor to the sea should become a part of the Polish state, because the interests of 1,600,000 Germans in East Prussia can be adequately protected by securing for them freedom of transit across the corridor, whereas it would be impossible to give an adequate outlet to the inhabitants of the new Polish state (numbering some 25,000,000) if this outlet had to be guaranteed across the territory of an alien and probably hostile Power. Finally, the fact must be recognized that 600,000 Poles in West Prussia would be any alternative plan remain under German rule.[12]

These proposals generated controversy at the conference, as Danzig was a mainly German city, with only about 10 percent Polish population.[13] Rather than accepting the initial proposal of the Polish Commission, the Big Four continued discussions on how to handle the corridor.

The Danzig question dragged on for many weeks as other parts of the Treaty of Versailles were being wrapped up. Opposition to the creation of the corridor, as proposed by the Commission, came mostly from British Prime Minister Lloyd George. He was greatly concerned that this plan would leave over two million Germans living in Poland.[14]

In April 1919, a Free City of Danzig was being floated as a compromise to granting Polish direct sovereignty over the major port city. On April 22, the Big Four agreed in principle to creation of the free city.[15] In May, the terms for the Free City of Danzig were laid out. It would be placed in customs union with Poland, ensuring that Poland had free use of its waterways and docks, while asserting Polish control of the rail facilities, but the city would be placed under the control of a High Commissioner under the protection of the League of Nations.[16] The Free City of Danzig was set up in the Treaty of Versailles and created in 1920.[17] This would, however, be far from the end of the story of this important port city's political status.

Two portions of Poland's border with East Prussia were granted the right for a plebiscite in the final plan, similar to the plebiscites proposed for Schleswig. The area around Allenstein (today known as Olsztyn) voted in 1920 to remain in Germany by a huge margin, 363,000 to 8,000.[18] The second area, around Marienwerder, which included the sole rail line from Warsaw to Danzig, voted overwhelmingly as well to remain in Germany in 1920.[19] These votes created final borders for the German exclave of East Prussia to remain slightly larger than the areas which had been initially proposed for East Prussia in the Black Book.

One other portion of the proposed Polish border with Germany posed problems, this being in the region of Upper Silesia, centered around Breslau (now known as Wrocław). The Inquiry had recommended this region remain mostly in Germany, due to its large German population, especially in the city of Breslau. The Inquiry border followed the linguistic line as best as possible. However, the Poles desired control of the entire region; Upper Silesia was not only a major industrial area but also possessed huge coal deposits. The Commission on Polish Affairs granted the region to Poland in its entirety, due to a Polish majority of 65 percent.[20] This contrasted with the proposed division of the region in the Black Book, which acknowledged that the western portions of Silesia were overwhelmingly populated by Germans. The British objected to the total transfer of Upper Silesia in high level negotiations in Paris, and finally it was determined that the region should receive a plebiscite, which occurred in 1921. The Council of the League of Nations arbitrated the final border based upon a plebiscite wherein over 700,000 votes were cast for union with Germany, while about 470,000 were cast for Poland.[21] This resulted in partition, with Germany receiving the western two-thirds. The boundary cut through the middle of an integrated economic region, thus causing both economic problems and great resentment on both the German and Polish sides for not receiving the entire territory.[22] After World War II, all of Upper Silesia would pass to Poland, and the large German population was expelled into a much smaller German state.

Not only did Poland provide significant challenges to the peacemakers in creating borders to the west with Germany, but due to the fluid political conditions to Poland's east, the challenges there were also immense, principally due to the ongoing Bolshevik Revolution and Russian Civil War. The Polish Commission was not able to address the eastern borders until the waning days of the peace conference. At the end of 1919, the Curzon Line, named after British Lord Curzon, who was instrumental in shaping this line, was proposed.[23] By this point, the American presence at the conference had disintegrated, illness having sent President Wilson home along with most of his entourage; thus the American experts were not involved in this decision. Poland refuted the Curzon Line, and the resulting Polish-Soviet War enabled Poland to gain a border far to the east of the Curzon Line, in the resulting Treaty of Riga.

Creating a large state like Poland out of the ashes of three empires proved immensely challenging for the experts at the Paris Peace Conference. Men such as Isaiah Bowman reached their positions through difficult closed-door negotiations, which were then adopted by the Big Four. These final positions were reached, not so much through answering the questions of idealism, national rights or historical justice, as through the interests in containing a potentially resurgent Germany and the new menace of the Soviet Union. Intense criticism of these territorial settlements followed. The Polish Corridor was widely derided in Germany, and became one of the most frequently criticized of the territorial settlements created in any of the treaties at the peace conference.[24] There was no way to draw a border through this region without creating population islands. It was not a lack of cartographic data, but the sheer problem of having to choose between dividing Germany in two or not giving Poland sea access, that made drawing these frontiers so difficult and that led to further bloodshed over them in ensuing decades.

In the end, it was more the fact that Poland was created than what the exact boundaries were that has held such significance in European history, post–World War I. The German perception of unfair borders, coupled with the French and British commitment to Poland's security, were central factors in the outbreak of World War II. Although Germany and the Soviet Union divided Poland, and later each occupied the entire country during portions of the war, Poland did reemerge after World War II, but with boundaries quite different from those effected after World War I. Rather than drawing borders based on ethnicity or other Wilsonian principles, the USSR unilaterally moved Poland westward, setting its eastern boundary near the Curzon Line and moving the western border to the Oder and Neisse Rivers. East Prussia, Upper Silesia and Danzig were integrated into Poland, and millions of Germans fled westward, while Poles in the east, especially around Lviv (in modern Ukraine), also fled west into the new Poland to escape living in the USSR. Today, Poland occupies these Soviet-drawn lines that encompass many areas envisioned by the Inquiry as part of Poland, but within an overall border that is quite different from either that envisioned in the Black Book or drawn at the Paris Peace Conference.

LITHUANIA—A POLISH UNION?

Poland's historic partner kingdom, Lithuania, received a less definitive treatment by the American Inquiry scholars and would face a much more skeptical audience than Poland at the peace conference. Around the same time as its Baltic neighbors (see chapter 3), Lithuania declared independence from the Russian Empire on February 16, 1918. It faced similar challenges to Latvia and Estonia due to its small size, but further complications also arose from a large mixture of population with ethnic Poles and Jews in the areas Lithuania claimed.

A separate Lithuanian state was considered as part of the American plan for peace, but it was also proposed that Lithuania may have been best off in a union with Poland, similar to the medieval Polish-Lithuanian state. The combined state was the preference of the Inquiry, as noted in the Black Book:

> It is recommended that a union of Poland and Lithuania be effected, if possible, with boundaries as shown on map 6.
>
> Poland and Lithuania are bound together by so many historic ties and common economic interests that their former political union, lasting for many centuries, should be restored. Lithuania is not strong enough to stand alone.
>
> The suggested union is universally desired by the Poles, and the Lithuanians could probably be brought to accept it if the terms of the union guaranteed full equality between their state and Poland, and if they were favored in the settlement of the chief dispute between them and Poland. The dispute related to the governments of Vilna, Grodno, and Minsk, which were historically and ethnically Lithuanian, but which have long since been denationalized and more and more polonized. If the union depended upon it the Poles would probably concede these territories to Lithuania.[25]

Clearly there were many challenges associated with this union, which led the Inquiry to also propose a backup plan of a separate Lithuanian state, a state, which did emerge, although with much smaller borders than those envisioned by the American proposal (see Figure 4.1):

> It is recommended that, if this union is not effected, Poland and Lithuania be established as mutually independent states, with boundaries not as shown on map 6, but adjusted to the ethnic facts in the Vilna-Grodno-Minsk district.
>
> If a union of Poland and Lithuania cannot be brought about an acrimonious dispute as to the three governments mentioned above will be developed between the two states.[26]

Although the Poles were enthusiastic about a union, mainly due to their much larger size and population, ensuring their ability to dominate the union, the Lithuanians favored the creation of their own separate state.

More than anything, the Lithuanians strove to have Vilnius as their capital. This city, however, had a Jewish majority, and was also greatly desired by the leaders of Poland. The Inquiry was well aware of the complexity of the area, as reflected in the Black Book. However, strong American support for Poland at the peace conference, compounded by a lack of interest by other parties, made the Lithuanian case difficult. The Lithuanian issue was almost totally ignored in meetings of the Big Four, where concerns in the former-Russian realms received little attention. By the summer of 1919, the Great Powers offered some political support, and Lithuania emerged as a separate state, without borders defined clearly in any of the postwar agreements.

The final frontiers between Poland and Lithuania, like many of the borders drawn in Eastern Europe, were shaped through conflict rather than the peace treaties. The Treaty of Riga, between Poland and the Soviet Union, eventually set an international border for Lithuania that allotted much of the original Lithuanian claim to Poland, including the Lithuanian claimed capital of Vilnius. The international community viewed the Polish seizure as illegal, but the constant disputes between the states, along with Lithuanian disputes with Germany over the border between Lithuania and East Prussia, led to Lithuania establishing insecure boundaries throughout the 1920s.[27] Polish-Lithuanian ties were so strained in Paris and the conflicts that followed that the two states did not maintain any diplomatic relations for fifteen years after the peace conference.[28]

Along with its Baltic neighbors, Lithuania was seized by the Soviet Union and incorporated as a constituent republic of the USSR during World War II. Stalin adjusted the borders of Lithuania to include Vilnius and other areas seized by Poland in the 1920s, but claimed by Lithuania at the Paris Peace Conference. However, other areas envisioned for Lithuania were instead given to Belarussia, including Minsk, which serves as independent Belarus' capital today. Lithuania, along with its Baltic neighbors of Latvia and Estonia, exited the USSR in 1990 prior to the dissolution of the entire Soviet state. The Soviet-imposed borders remain in place today, thus giving Lithuania a very different geography than that imagined by the American Inquiry or that which emerged in the years following the Paris Peace Conference.

CZECHOSLOVAKIA

Emerging from the First World War, Czechoslovakia would remain a fixture in the center of the map of Europe for 75 years before breaking apart. Czechoslovakia was declared as a new state on October 28, 1918, just as the Austro-Hungarian Empire collapsed. If Poland's champion was the United States, the champion of Czechoslovakia was in no small measure the Czech leader himself, Tomas Masaryk. Masaryk had been an advocate for the freedom of the peoples of Austria-Hungary and he held widespread acclaim in Paris. Despite this, several areas proposed for the new Czechoslovak state would cause problems, both in Paris and later in history, including the acquisition of the Sudetenland, and the settlement of an agreed border with Poland to the north and Hungary to the south.

The Inquiry was strongly supportive of the creation of Czechoslovakia (see Figure 4.2):

It is recommended that there be established a Czecho-Slovak state, with boundaries as shown on maps 8 and 16.

The establishment of a Czecho-Slovak state is now a *fait accompli*. Its governmental machinery has been organized, and it only remains to fix the conditions of its existence and of its frontiers.

In Austria, the boundary follows the historical frontier of the Bohemian crownlands, with slight rectifications to conform with the Polish frontier in German Silesia and to exclude the Polish district around Teschen.

Such a frontier would include more than 2,500,000 Germans, but the economic interests of these Germans bind them to the Czecho-Slovak state. Their own sentiment is reported to be chiefly in favor of the proposed union, provided they are guaranteed minority rights and economic equality.

In Hungary, the recommended frontier runs south of the linguistic border and includes more than 500,000 Magyars. There is thus afforded, along a short strip of the Danube, a commercial outlet of great importance to a landlocked state. Moreover, were the ethnic lines to be followed it would cross at right angles the main northern tributary valleys of the Danube in this region, and seriously derange the economic relations of the people.[29]

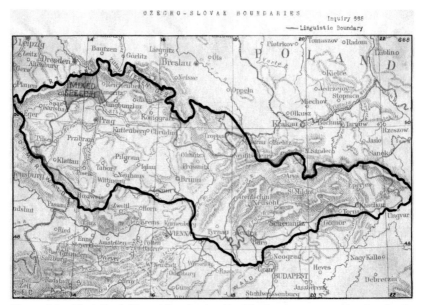

Figure 4.2.   *Black Book Map of Czechoslovakia: The Inquiry proposed borders for the new Czechoslovak state that extended beyond the linguistic boundaries of Czech and Slovak speakers in many areas. Economic and strategic factors clearly played important roles in the definition of the new state's borders. It is also noteworthy that the Black Book map makes no differentiation between the Czech and Slovak halves of the country, although a major linguistic divide should actually be shown running directly through the middle of the proposed state. (Map from JHU Bowman Papers MS 58 13.13)*

Clearly, the Inquiry accepted that Czechoslovakia was to come into being, as the state had already organized itself well ahead of the start of the conference. However, the Black Book directly acknowledges that the state, as proposed by Masaryk, would certainly not meet the Wilsonian principle of self-determination, as large groups of both Germans and Hungarians would find themselves within this new state. The Inquiry instead relied on economic factors as the basis for the borders of Czechoslovakia, especially regarding the inclusion of Sudetenland and the extension of Slovak territory deep into the Hungarian Plain to the south.

Even more worrisome, there was no discussion of whether there should be one state, or separate ones for the Czechs and Slovaks. Although they spoke different dialects (as understood at the time), the American documents of the period suggest that these were not separate languages.[30] Also, the Czechs had been part of the Austrian half of the previous Austro-Hungarian Empire, while the Slovaks were part of Hungarian half, thus meaning the two groups had lived under quite different political conditions prior to the Paris Peace Conference. Over time, serious strains would indeed develop between the Czechs and Slovaks.

The western borders of Czechoslovakia with Germany were barely discussed at the conference and not at all in meetings of the Big Four. The German delegation did not even make a case to have them transferred to Germany. Thus, with little fanfare or attention, the Sudetenland, one of Hitler's prime targets a mere fifteen years later, was passed to Czechoslovakia, despite its overwhelming German majority. This region had been a part of the Austrian empire, and not a part of Germany, so it would have been unlikely that any other solution for this territory would be considered. The border with Poland would prove slightly more complex in ensuing negotiations.

Prior to the conference, the Inquiry anticipated a dispute between Poland and Czechoslovakia over the Teschen region. The Black Book called for a boundary drawn by linguistic factors, rather than ceding the whole area to Czechoslovakia based upon historical claims from the prior Kingdom of Bohemia:

> In the duchy of Teschen the boundary follows the Polish-Czech linguistic line, disregarding Czech claims to the whole of this rich little territory on a weak basis of "historic rights."[31]

In general, the Inquiry proposals for Czechoslovakia were based on historic borders located within Austria-Hungary. Based on these, Teschen would be placed in Czechoslovakia, but the area was ethnically mixed, and therefore integrating parts of it into Polish Galicia made more sense based on Wilsonian principles. Teschen not only was ethnically mixed, but held large supplies of coal, a key strategic resource. No final agreement on the status of Teschen was reached in Paris, but in 1920 it was agreed to divide the region between the countries, as envisioned by the Inquiry, with the Czechs gaining the western two-thirds including the main coal mines, while Poland gained the eastern third, including the town of Teschen and most of the Polish population.[32]

While most of the borders in the Czech half of the state were based on historic boundaries, the southern border for the Slovak half was based neither on historic nor ethnic factors, which would have been key to implementing a Wilsonian principle-based peace. Rather, the Inquiry proposed a line that would give Czechoslovakia access to the Danube River, the principal waterway and conduit of commerce in Central Europe, at Bratislava. The regions transferred from Hungary included areas well south of the linguistic line between Slovaks and Hungarians. This settlement passed approximately 750,000 Hungarians to Czechoslovakia once the boundary set in the Treaty of Trianon was drawn.[33]

In the end, Czechoslovakia inherited a significant minority problem, with about 35 percent of the population being neither Czech nor Slovak. Not only did they have a large Hungarian population in the south, but there was an enormous German population of over 3.2 million (including 1.7 million Sudeten Germans) and a smattering of Ruthenians and Poles (for a discussion of Czechoslovakia's acquisition of Ruthenia, see chapter 5).[34] The new borders of the state could not be justified on the grounds of self-determination, but only based upon strategic concerns.[35] The Czech core area differed greatly from the Slovak and Ruthene regions, and the Germans in the border zones with Germany all created centripetal forces that pulled at the state from the very start.[36] Almost by fiat, and thanks to their skill in interacting with the Great Powers and especially the Big Four themselves, the Czechoslovak government gained their territory with almost no high-level discussions in Paris. After being dismantled by Germany during World War II, Czechoslovakia reemerged with slightly altered eastern borders in 1945 to survive until 1994. In the long run it would prove that the differences between Czechs and Slovaks were much greater than acknowledged in the early 20th century. On January 1, 1994, Czechoslovakia ceased to exist, and the Velvet Revolution (so-called for its peacefulness) led to the emergence of two states, the Czech Republic and Slovakia in its place.

YUGOSLAVIA

Czechoslovakia was not the only new multiethnic state born from the crumbling empires of Central and Eastern Europe. Another state, Yugoslavia, emerged at the same time and with a much larger and more diverse population. In hindsight, the creation of a Yugoslav state seems naïve at best. However, the calls for the creation of such a state were especially strong in the early 20th century, while there was very little talk of creating separate states for the peoples of this troubled region. Although the United States was the most impassioned of the Great Powers in its call for the creation of Yugoslavia, the British and French were also strong supporters of creating a Yugoslav state. Only Italy opposed its creation along the lines called for by the United States, finding a strong state to its east undesirable and because Italy coveted many areas envisioned for Yugoslavia for itself. This opposition would lead to dramatic consequences in the negotiation of their mutual border.

The idea of creating a union for the south Slavs arose prior to the First World War; however, support among the more northerly groups of these Slavs (principally Slovenes and Croats) was dilute until the chaotic collapse of the Austro-Hungarian Empire in 1918.[37] At this time, the national councils of the three main south Slavic groups gained the upper hand over their less organized opponents and declared the creation of the Kingdom of the Serbs, Croats and Slovenes on December 1, 1918.[38] This country quickly acquired the short-form moniker Yugoslavia. Prior to World War I, the main aim of most south Slavic peoples was to keep out the Turks. With only the Serbs pushing for a Yugoslav state, the decision led to Serbian territory growing by two-thirds at war's end to include these other peoples.[39] The Serbs attained the upper hand over the Croats within this new polity and immediately set out to define what territory it should include. They based their claims on language, and decided that Yugoslavia should include all the lands up to Carniola (Slovenia) where Slavic speakers resided.[40]

Not only did Yugoslavia unite people speaking several different languages—Serbo-Croatian, Slovenian, Macedonian, and Albanian—but it also united peoples of differing religions. The union was hampered by internal conflict from the outset by the divisions between Catholic Croats and Slovenes, Muslims in the Bosnian regions and in Kosovo, and the majority Eastern Orthodox populations further south in Serbia, Montenegro, parts of Bosnia, and Macedonia. Based on the Wilsonian principle of self-determination, this dramatic diversity hardly seems to fit with either a linguistic or religious approach to defining the Yugoslav nation.

Despite these complications, the American Inquiry scholars quickly embraced the idea of crafting a Yugoslav state, rather than a series of smaller states in the western Balkans. This new state would be unlike any entity already existing in the region. The Black Book plan specified:

> That an independent federated Jugo-Slav state be established, to consist of Serbia, Montenegro, and the Serbo-Croat-Slovene territory within former Austria Hungary.[41]

In general, the Black Book called for a border along the linguistic divides, but it acknowledged that the proposed borders would skew from these lines within both the Banat (see chapter 3 on Romania) and in the Istrian region along the Adriatic seacoast east of Venice.[42] Many of Serbia's extant borders were preserved in the new Yugoslav boundaries as well, including Serbia's control over northern Macedonia (today's Republic of Macedonia), a region containing large populations speaking a different Slavic language and also large numbers of Albanians. After the two devastating Balkan Wars that preceded the First World War, the boundaries of the Balkans had already undergone significant changes, which the American plan tried to avoid altering in any significant fashion. The 1913 Serbian borders with Romania, Bulgaria, Greece and Albania were to remain in place in the American plan for the new state.[43] However, Serbia and Montenegro would disappear as separate states, leading to the elimination of one of the longest-standing borders in this otherwise fluid region.

The Americans anticipated one major problem with the boundaries they were proposing for the new state, which was due to the division of the Albanian population between Yugoslavia and Albania. Little did the American planners know that eighty years after the peace conference, the very region they proposed including in Yugoslavia—Kosovo—would erupt with a major ethnic conflict that would involve the United States once again in the region. The Black Book plan called for a League of Nations mandatory regime in Kosovo, to protect the rights of Albanians in Yugoslavia, rather than calling for an adjustment in the frontier to include Kosovo in Albania:

> It is recommended that the tentative suggestion be considered of uniting the "High" Albanians of Northern Albania with their own kin in western Serbia and southeastern Montenegro, and placing this homogenous group of tribes in a self-governing unit under Jugo-Slavia as a mandatory

of the League of Nations, with the explicit right reserved to it of appeal to the League of Nations in case of oppression; and of altering the former Serbian and Montenegrin boundaries, as fixed in 1913...

On the other hand it appears unwise to grant Jugo-Slavia complete sovereignty in Northern Albania, since Serbs and Albanians at present dislike and distrust each other. Doubtless in time the process of absorption of the Albanian population would follow the course it is now running, but the process should not be violently stimulated, and the Albanians should certainly be protected against abuse.[44]

In the clarity of hindsight, clearly the Inquiry underestimated the "dislike and distrust" between Albanians and Serbs, and certainly overestimated the chances of Albanian absorption into the Serb population.

Albania made claims to Kosovo at the conference, stating the region had been in Albanian hands since "time immemorial," while Serbs had only arrived in the 7th century. These sorts of historical arguments did not play well with President Wilson or the American delegation. However, Kosovo would not end up being an important issue at the conference because the Great Powers saw no reason to extend the borders of Albania in any direction.[45] The lack of interest in the Albanian cause was clearly related to the negative views held by the peacemakers towards the Albanian people, due to factors including religion and level of development (for a discussion on the proposals for Albania put forth by the United States see chapter 5).

Yugoslavia did receive several territorial settlements different from those proposed by the Americans. The Committee for the Study of Territorial Questions Relating to Rumania and Yugoslavia was set up in February 1919, to propose the exact delimitation of new frontiers, and it presented its initial report on April 6, 1919.[46] In the report, the Committee proposed several adjustments beyond just combining Serbia and Montenegro with the Austrian regions of Bosnia, Herzegovina, Croatia and Carniola (Slovenia). There was a proposed adjustment in the border with Bulgaria, and rectifications were also considered along the border with Austria, as a mixed population resided in the Klagenfurt Basin along that proposed border. However, with disagreements between Italy and other Committee members, the Italian frontier was left for negotiation directly among the Big Four.

The only major differences with the American plans could be seen in the Committee's report on the border with Bulgaria, where the Americans recommended that the old border be preserved, while the Committee recommended four additions to Yugoslavia, and minor changes in the ethnically mixed region along the Slovene-Austrian border. With the complex mixture of Austrians and Slovenes in this area, the American, British and French members of the Committee called for a plebiscite or other local arrangement to determine the disposition of the area, while the Italians, who in general opposed the Yugoslavs throughout the conference, called for the area remaining in Austria. Eventually, the Klagenfurt issue was drawn into bigger disputes regarding the Italian-Yugoslav border. Yugoslavia worried they would lose the plebiscite if one was called; however, following a meeting of the Big Four in which the members and experts crawled around on the floor looking at a huge ethnic map of the area (likely from the Inquiry's collections), it was decided to go forward with a vote.[47] The plebiscite was held in 1920, resulting in Klagenfurt remaining in Austria, much as the Yugoslavs had expected would happen.[48] In this one part of the drawing of the Yugoslav border, the rule of self-determination was able to hold sway, although in other areas, this would be far from the case.

Following the conference, concern was voiced as to the long-term stability of this multiethnic polity, a land that was a "curious hodge-podge" of nationalities, languages, religions and alphabets.[49] Writing in 1921, Charles Seymour presciently remarked, "Jugo-Slavia includes comparatively few outsiders, but the differences between Croats, Slovenes, and Serbs do not promise a tranquil future."[50] Other scholars pointed to the same divides among these three main groups.[51] Chief Geographer Isaiah Bowman also noted the difficulties surrounding the southernmost regions in Macedonia, noting that it remained unclear whether or not Macedonia could have been created as a separate state, but that the Macedonian question would continue to haunt the region for many years.[52] Based on hindsight, it is clear that even these descriptions were understated. Yugoslavia unraveled twice. First, during World War II the Croat and Bosnian Ustache militias unleashed havoc and widespread genocide against the Serbs before the country was restored to similar borders at the end of the war. The second breakup continues to evolve even now, beginning with Slovenia's independence in 1991. Since that time, Croatia, Bosnia and Herzegovina, Macedonia, Montenegro and finally Kosovo have all broken off from Serbia. The final borders that will emerge here remain uncertain to this day, with fewer than half of the world's states recognizing Kosovo at the time of this writing (the United States was one of the first countries to recognize Kosovo as an independent state).

DRAWING A BORDER BETWEEN ALLIES—
ITALY & YUGOSLAVIA

The biggest test of President Wilson's principles at the Paris Peace Conference erupted over a small port city on the eastern shore of the Adriatic Sea. The conflict that broke out within the Big Four over Fiume (now Rijeka, Croatia) almost led to the collapse of the entire Paris Peace Conference. Had the Italians kept their territorial appetites within reasonable bounds, that major conflict would have been easily averted.[53] The disputes that arose over Fiume and the two contested regions just up and down the coast from it, Istria and Dalmatia, led to a major split among the Allies and tested the resolve of the American delegation to adhere to the principles and plans they brought to Paris. Unlike most territories contested at the conference, where parties on opposing sides in the war argued over a territorial disposition, this conflict pitted Italy against Yugoslavia, who had fought side-by-side during the war.

Prior to the First World War, the regions of Istria and Dalmatia sat within the Austrian portion of the Austro-Hungarian Empire, while the city of Fiume, located between these two regions, served as Hungary's main port and only outlet to the sea. These regions, formerly a part of the defunct Venetian Republic, had long been under control of the Austrian Empire. The peoples living throughout the Croatian lands of Hungary had been supportive of the cause of the Austro-Hungarian Empire during World War I, as they feared Italy's desire to annex much of their territory.[54] These fears were well founded.

On the Istrian Peninsula, just west of Fiume, about 147,000 Italians lived on the eastern shores of the Adriatic Sea between Trieste and Pola, with Slavic peoples residing in the mountainous regions beyond.[55] Other than these areas, Italians never constituted a major population on the east coast of the Adriatic Sea at any point in history.[56] The division of peoples in this area constituted a complex problem. The linguistic boundary through the area was such that the small Istrian Peninsula would need to be divided between Italy and Yugoslavia and the two cities of Trieste and Fiume would be left as small Italian exclaves within a Yugoslav-dominated region.

More than just the nationality issue came into play for Italy. The Italians had long considered the Adriatic an Italian sea, dating back to the Venetian and even Roman periods.[57] They felt control of the sea was vital to their security and prosperity. For these reasons, Italy gained territorial concessions that included both the entire Istrian Peninsula and parts of Dalmatia in the secret 1915 Treaty of London with France and the United Kingdom (see Figure 4.3). This treaty made Serbia feel sold out by her al-

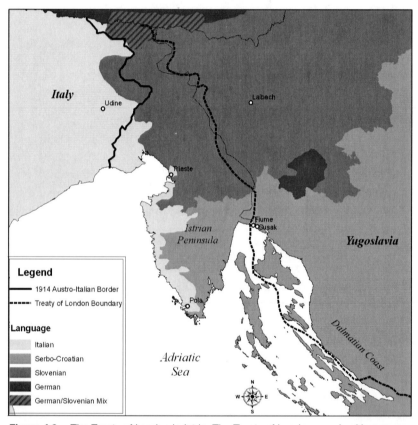

Figure 4.3.   *The Treaty of London in Istria: The Treaty of London promised large areas inhabited by speakers of Serbo-Croatian and Slovenian to Italy. Many of the Dalmatian islands and part of the Dalmatian coast were also promised to Italy. It is noteworthy that the city of Fiume lies just across the Treaty of London line, inside areas promised to Yugoslavia, but by the opening of the peace conference, Italy was also claiming this city. (Cartography by the author)*

lies, and other than the United States, there was a strong favoritism toward Italy by the other Great Powers prior to the start of the peace conference.[58] However, the port city of Fiume was not promised to Italy in the treaty; following the war Italy decided to lay claim to that city as well.

The Inquiry faced a difficult decision in creating the American proposal for Istria. As the United States was not a party to the Treaty of London and explicitly ruled out such treaties in the Fourteen Points, the Inquiry was free to develop a plan that would correspond closely to Wilson's principles. Three of the Fourteen Points related to the region and served as guides for the initial American proposal to be delivered at the conference:

I. Open covenants of peace, openly arrived at, after which there shall be no private international understandings of any kind but diplomacy shall proceed always frankly and in the public view.

IX. A readjustment of the frontiers of Italy should be effected along clearly recognizable lines of nationality.

XI. Rumania, Serbia, and Montenegro should be evacuated; occupied territories restored; Serbia accorded free and secure access to the sea; and the relations of the several Balkan states to one another determined by friendly counsel along historically established lines of allegiance and nationality; and international guarantees of the political and economic independence and territorial integrity of the several Balkan states should be entered into.[59]

Point I clearly voided the Treaty of London from the American viewpoint. Point IX gave the Inquiry guidance as to where to place the border. Point XI reflected an earlier reality, and so the Inquiry had to reinterpret it to include the new reality of Yugoslavia, a state that in the new structure fit with Wilson's view that relations among the Balkan states should be determined by "friendly counsel." The acceptance of these points by the Allied states negated the Treaty of London entirely, in the view of senior Americans delegates to Paris. Clearly, the Inquiry would have to base its proposal on a new border between Italy and Yugoslavia that ran through Austro-Hungarian territory along ethnic or linguistic lines.

Knowing that Istria would prove problematic at the conference, the Black Book laid out two options for a new border between the Italy and

Yugoslavia, both of which, it acknowledged, would fail to fully follow a linguistic line, and would demonstrate favoritism toward the Italian position (see Figure 4.4):

> The Jugo-Slav boundary of the Istria-Isonzo region is the subject of hot dispute because both the Jugo-Slavs and the Italians are eager for the possession of the eastern Adriatic littoral and its ports. The commercial and strategic advantages accruing to the possessor are obvious.
>
> The proposed boundary coincides in general with the main watershed of the Carnic and Julian Alps, and follows the crest of the high ridges forming the backbone of the Istrian peninsula. It gives to Italy all of that portion of the Isonzo basin and of the eastern Adriatic coast to which she has any valid claim, together with as much of the hinterland, peopled by Slavs, as it vitally needed on economic grounds. It gives to the Jugo-Slavs part of the Istrian coast and all of the Dalmatian coast and archipelago claimed by Italy, with a fine series of harbors from Fiume southward.
>
> ...The Jugo-Slavs would be left in undisturbed possession of a stretch of coast upon which their hopes have centered for years, and where the Italian claim to majorities is unsubstantiated, except in the case of several coast towns, such as Fiume and Zara—there is a small Italian majority in Fiume proper, but a small Croat majority if the suburb of Susak, in fact a part of Fiume, be added.
>
> The retention of Fiume by Jugo-Slavia is vital to the interests of the latter, and likewise assures to the more remote hinterland, including Austria and Hungary, the advantages of two competing ports under the control of different nations.[60]

Even this proposal gives Italy more land than suggested in Point IX of the Fourteen Points. However, anticipating Italian demands, the Inquiry clearly decided it best to offer the Italians a modest compromise, since the American proposal removes all the Dalmatian areas claimed by Italy in the Treaty of London, as well as half of the Istrian Peninsula, which the treaty fully granted to Italy. On the issue of Fiume, the Inquiry felt that any compromise would violate Wilson's principles. The Inquiry studies point out that if Fiume's suburbs, such as Susak, are included in the population count, the city in fact has a Croat majority rather than an Italian one. Austria-Hungary had relied on Trieste and Fiume as its only major deepwater ports. Following its demise, most of the successor states

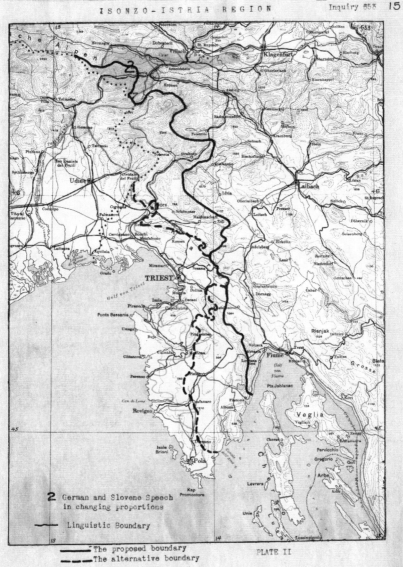

Figure 4.4. *Black Book Map of Istria: The Inquiry map of Istria provides two border proposals, unlike other areas in the book, which only give a single proposal. The Inquiry staff was aware that this region would prove difficult in negotiations and therefore gave the President more options. Both American proposed lines give Italy areas beyond the linguistic divide, but far less than the territory promised in the Treaty of London. (Map from JHU Bowman Papers MS 58 13.13)*

were left landlocked, including not only Austria and Hungary, but also Czechoslovakia. If Trieste was granted to Italy and Fiume to Yugoslavia, there would be multiple deepwater port options for these countries that were not under a single authority. To do otherwise would place all of these landlocked states at the whim of Italy, a country with which many were unlikely to have strong and stable relations following the conflict. The Inquiry proposal gave Italy as much of its strategic objective as they felt was warranted without jeopardizing the economic and strategic needs of Yugoslavia. In the end, the American delegation decided it was best to base territorial decisions in Istria and Dalmatia not on the ethnic makeup of an individual port, but rather on the entire population of the port and its hinterlands.[61] Under this guideline, the Italian claim to Fiume based on nationality became void. However, it should be noted that the Inquiry's views were also shaded slightly by the ethnic maps and data they used, much of which was created by an ethnic Serb, Jovan Cvijic, whose materials tended to favor the Yugoslav view, with which the Inquiry generally sided.[62]

The Americans knew they faced a difficult decision heading into negotiations on Istria, Dalmatia and Fiume. The dispute between Italy and Yugoslavia seemed almost intractable because the ethnic, cultural and strategic lines in the Adriatic did not correspond, and even finding a balance between them was difficult.[63] Despite this, the Inquiry provided President Wilson with two possible borders in Istria between Italy and Yugoslavia to present to the delegations at Paris. Both are shown on the Black Book map used each day by President Wilson during the contentious negotiations over this region.

Upon arrival at the Paris Peace Conference, both Italy and Yugoslavia immediately pressed their claims to Istria, Dalmatia and especially Fiume. In one-on-one meetings with the other major powers, both sides relied heavily on economic considerations, with Italy claiming that Yugoslavia had no economic need for the port, while the Yugoslavs argued the hinterlands of Slovenia and Croatia needed this port to remain economically vibrant.[64] Both sides also presented historical justifications for their claims to Fiume, since the population divide was too close to use national data convincingly. The Italians also resorted to a cultural argument when stating their case, reporting that even in areas such as Dalmatia, where they were the ethnic minority, Italian cultural dominance was strong enough to overcome this.[65] This was a dubious claim, based on the foods and architecture of the region, especially when considered in relation to President Wilson's new principles, which clearly supported factors such as language and religion.

The conference focused on the German treaty before moving on to Austria and Hungary. This delayed a confrontation over Fiume until after much work had been accomplished by the Big Four. However, no greater conflict would emerge among the Big Four than the split between President Wilson and Prime Minister Orlando over Fiume.[66]

The negotiations on Italy's frontiers with the former Austro-Hungarian Empire began in mid-April, 1919. In his initial presentation of Italian claims, Prime Minister Orlando recognized the United States was not party to the Treaty of London, yet he presented Italian claims that included all lands granted in the treaty in both Istria and Dalmatia, along with the claim to Fiume, despite the fact that it was outside the line agreed to with Britain and France in 1915.[67] The Italian claims presented by Orlando were based on both national and strategic concerns, he explained, as Italy not only wished to unite her people within the state, but also to ensure the safety of the Adriatic. This necessitated Italy's control of the Dalmatian islands and part of its coast, as the Austrian navy had employed this as a shield to launch raids on Italy during the war.

President Wilson resisted the Italian claims immediately, and instead presented the lines through Istria created by the Inquiry as possible frontiers between Italy and Yugoslavia. Wilson argued that it was unreasonable for Italy to support the nationality-based frontiers in the German treaty, but to then expect a different set of principles to be applied to the Austrian and Hungarian treaties.[68] Wilson expected that all treaties would fit within his ideals for the new diplomacy and world order he was helping to shape, and he would not be convinced otherwise when concerned with the Italian border. Italy's signing of an armistice based on the Fourteen Points voided their previous agreements under the Treaty of London, in the view of Wilson and his delegation. President Wilson stated that it was completely inconsistent with the new order of international relations to place Fiume in Italy.[69] Wilson further argued that Italy needed to stay out of the Balkans, as he believed that Great Power interference in the Balkans had been the primary catalyst of the recent war, a fair point due to the war breaking out in nearby Bosnia, and therefore these states should be left alone by the Great Powers as much as possible. On these frontiers Wilson remained adamant:

> If this did not suffice, then two orders would exist—the old and the new. In the right hand would be the new order and in the left hand the old order. We could not drive two horses at once. The people of the United States of America would repudiate it. They were disgusted with the old order. Not only the American people but the people of the whole world were tired of the old system and they would not put up with Governments that supported it.[70]

Wilson plainly laid out his case that Italy would have to drop the claims to Fiume and Dalmatia entirely. He seemed convinced that any compromise on this issue threatened his entire program of peace, and that without the settlement following the ideals under which the United States went to war, there would be no chance of American ratification of the treaties of peace.

In further meetings between the Big Four on April 20, the Italians showed no sign of compromise. Prime Minister Orlando argued that "the fact that Fiume may not be given to Italy would be extremely fatal just as much to the interests of Italy as to the peace of the world."[71] This held no sway with the rest of the council, despite Italian threats that they would consider fighting Yugoslavia to gain the port. President Wilson stood by his original offer, arguing that without the Treaty of London, Italy would receive its natural boundaries and the redemption of the Italian population. On April 22, the Italians presented their border proposal, including Fiume, to the council. Orlando expected that Wilson would capitulate to the Italian demands and at the same time found himself unable to pull any of them back, facing the fall of his coalition government, as the nationalists in Italy were unwilling to compromise on this issue.[72] Thus, domestic politics in Italy and the United States drove the Big Four toward disaster.

The Big Four met without Italy later on April 22. At this point, President Wilson presented a new compromise for Fiume. He proposed that Fiume be established as a free city, along similar lines to the situation created for Danzig.[73] The Italians presented one final offer on April 23, a practical repeat of their previous one and a nonstarter for the other major powers, while rejecting the idea of a free state outright.[74] At this point the Italians left Paris, nearly causing the conference to collapse. However, this did not stop the other delegations from looking for a solution to the Fiume and Dalmatia issue. Wilson proposed a plebiscite be organized along the entire Dalmatian coast, with the idea of a Free City of Fiume also being created that could later vote whether to join Italy, join Yugoslavia or remain independent.[75] This plebiscite would adhere closely to the ideals of self-determination, but also would be difficult to set up fairly, with the militant positions and provocations coming from both the Italian and Yugoslav governments concerning the region.

By late May, the Italians returned to Paris. At this point, the other Great Powers presented their compromise plan to Italy. The proposal of the Allies was summed up as:

> The State of Fiume to be under the League of Nations, and to consist of a fairly large State… The State to be administered by the following: two representatives from Italy, one nominated by the State of Fiume, one nominated by the Jugo-Slavs, and one nominated by the other Great Powers.
>
> At the end of 15 years a plebiscite to be held, when the people would decide whether they would remain independent, or become Italian, or become Croatian.[76]

Under this plan, all of Dalmatia was to remain in the hands of Yugoslavia. This compromise plan was further elaborated upon at later meetings of the Big Four. The Italians accepted it in spirit, but with reservations.[77] However, domestic pressures in Italy remained too high to accept this compromise position for long. Although Italy did not abandon the conference again, by mid-June they were threatening to not sign the German treaty (the Treaty of Versailles), due to a lack of favorable settlement on Fiume and Dalmatia.[78]

Wilson's determination was not enough to bring forth an equitable settlement along this border. However, it is fair to term any amelioration from the Italian demands as due to the firm stance that Wilson took at the conference.[79] Wilson's efforts earned him widespread admiration in Yugoslavia, going so far as locals granting him the moniker "Uncle Wilson."[80]

In the 1920 Treaty of Rapallo, Italy and Yugoslavia finally reached a settlement on the status of Istria, Dalmatia and Fiume, greatly diminishing the rivalry between the two states that had erupted two years earlier.[81] Under the final settlement, Italy gained the entire Istrian Peninsula. Italy also gained a few islands of the Dalmatian archipelago, although many fewer than they claimed in the Treaty of London. Yugoslavia gained the entire Dalmatian coast and most of the islands. Fiume was established as a free city, with a final status to be determined later. The 1923 Treaty of Rome ended the Free City of Fiume, and the city joined Italy.[82] The Yugoslavs agreed to this settlement the following year, with Fiume's eastern suburb of Susak being granted to them as a new port.

These early disputes over the Adriatic took a major toll on Yugoslavia. Not only did the fledgling state need to integrate peoples of different languages and religions, but it also faced a lack of commercial outlets and ports, along with the costly military rivalry with Italy. The distractions of the territorial disputes made it very difficult for Yugoslavia to integrate fully. Its motivating purpose had been more opposition to rule by non-Slavs than one of peoples who felt united, and the Serbs took advantage of this to turn Yugoslavia into a Serb-dominated state.[83]

Both Fiume and Istria remained contested territories throughout the 1930s. The rise of fascism in Italy and later Croatia led to a readjustment of territory following World War II. The Yugoslav nationalists under Tito joined with the Allies and thus were able to annex large amounts of territory from Italy at the end of the war. The Yugoslavs gained Fiume and renamed it Rijeka. The city remains a major port in Croatia today. The Istrian Peninsula was also transferred to Yugoslavia and today lies mostly within Croatia, with the northernmost parts in Slovenia. If Italy had accepted less after World War I by accepting the "Wilson Line," it is unlikely that they would have lost the entire Istrian Peninsula after World War II.[84]

ROMANIA'S EASTERN FRONTIER

Romania would emerge from World War I with the largest territorial extent in its history. In the breakup of Hungary, Romania would expand dramatically to the northwest, borders it retains to this day. However, Romania would temporarily expand eastward into regions later annexed by the Soviet Union during World War II. The American peace plan called for the Romanian absorption of Bessarabia, modern-day Moldova (see Figure 4.5):

> It is recommended that the whole of Bessarabia be added to the Rumanian state.
>
> Bessarabia was once a part of Rumania (14th Century to 1812; 1856 to 1878), and is quite predominantly Rumanian in character. The idea of

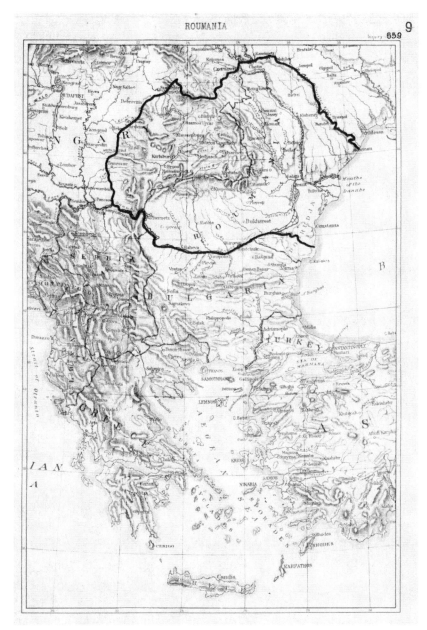

Figure 4.5. *Second Black Book Map of Romania: The Black Book called for the inclusion of all of Bessarbia in the Romanian state (areas seen in the northeastern corner of the proposed Romania, beyond the old Moldavian border with the Russian Empire), including areas with a Ukrainian majority. This includes almost all of modern Moldova and parts of Ukraine. (Map from JHU Bowman Papers MS 58 13.13)*

detaching the northern and southeastern corners (Khotin and Akkerman respectively) and giving them to the Ukraine is unwise, since it would break up a historic province and abandon a good natural frontier, the river Dneister, on account of relatively small Ukrainian colonies.[85]

Not only was Bessarbia to be added, but the Inquiry also called for the incorporation of half of Bucovina (an area now divided between Romanian Bucovina and Ukrainian Chernovisti) into the Romanian state:

> It is recommended that the ethnographical Rumanian part of Bukowina be added to the Rumanian state.
> Bukowina is divided into two main ethnographic regions. It is composed chiefly of the Ruthenian and Rumanian populations with a fairly well defined line of division, which is rather closely followed in maps 9 and 10.[86]

The ethno-linguistic makeup of Bessarbia worked in favor of the Romanians, as the Moldavian dialect was still clearly a dialect of Romanian. However, Bucovina and the coastal regions of Bessarbia along the Black Sea held large populations of Ukrainians. Bucovina sat at the easternmost point of Austrian territory, and was therefore to be handled in the discussions regarding the breakup of the Hapsburg Empire. However, Bessarbia constituted part of the Russian Empire, which caused much greater confusion for the peace conference attendees, with the Bolshevik Revolution and lack of Russian representation in Paris. The Romanians had occupied both regions in the waning days of the war and made a strong claim as soon as they arrived in Paris.

The Big Four spent very little time resolving the final settlement for these eastern regions. The Committee for the Study of Territorial Questions Relating to Rumania and Yugoslavia presented its report on Romanian frontiers on April 6, 1919, recommending the Romanian claims to Bucovina and Bessarbia be accepted exactly along the lines proposed by the Romanian government. The report noted that Bessarbia was of "Moldavian character" and should therefore be placed within Romania.[87] Bucovina was a little trickier, due to the mix of populations located there, as also reflected in the Black Book discussion on this region. However, the Committee recommended the entire region be transferred to Romania, minus a small Ruthene-populated area in the northwest that would result in 85,000 Ruthenians remaining outside

Romanian borders that would otherwise have been included under this plan.[88] These two additions would result in 1.9 million Romanians and 1.3 million other people being transferred to Romania.[89] Most of the non-Romanian population in the region consisted of Ukrainians and Ruthenians (most of whom now identify as Catholic Ukrainians).

In May, the Council of Foreign Ministers recommended the Committee report for Bucovina be accepted as part of the Austrian treaty.[90] There was no dissent among the Big Four to this border change. As Bessarabia lay within Russia, the *de facto* occupation of the territory led to its inclusion in Romania.

Following the war, Romania encountered problems in these eastern territories. Many in Bessarabia were opposed to Romanian rule, and the Romanian government feared Russia may try to take back Bessarabia.[91] These fears were certainly justified, as the Soviet Union did eventually subsume this territory, but not until the end of World War II. The USSR occupied both Bessarabia and the northern half of Bucovina. The Bucovinian area and the southern portions of Bessarabia were each added to Ukraine, while the rest of Bessarabia, along with a part of Ukraine across the Dneister River, became the Moldavian Soviet Socialist Republic. In the early 1990s, following the dissolution of the Soviet Union, the now independent Moldova discussed joining with Romania, but this never moved very far. The borders that exist in this region today stand in stark contrast to those drawn in Paris.

Clearly, many borders drawn in Paris have seen dramatic changes since the Paris Peace Conference. In some cases, borders directly proposed in the Black Book by the American delegation have disappeared, either because they did not follow the ethno-linguistic border (e.g., the Italian-Yugoslav border), they combined multiple groups in a single new state (e.g., Yugoslavia or Czechoslovakia), or outside events led to border changes and major shifts in populations (e.g., Poland's borders). In general, it can be concluded that the American Inquiry presented better options than those employed in some of these volatile areas, especially regarding the Italian-Yugoslav border. In other cases, it was a general naivety as to the best course of action for creating new states that led to future problems. Although there were more European states in 1919 than 1914, the peace treaties still created new multiethnic states and many miles of contentious new borders.

NOTES

1. Address of President Wilson to Congress, January 8, 1918. In Arthur Link. 1984. *The Papers of Woodrow Wilson, Volume 45*. Princeton: Princeton University Press. Pg. 536.

2. Robert Lord. 1921. "Poland," in *What Really Happened at Paris: The Story of the Peace Conference, 1918–1919 by American Delegates*, ed. Edward House. New York: Charles Scribner's Sons. Pg. 72.

3. Hugh Seton-Watson. 1977. *Nations and States: An Enquiry into the Origins of Nations and the Politics of Nationalism*. Boulder, CO: Westview Press. Pg. 129.

4. Lord, 1921. Pg. 71.

5. Leon Dominian. 1915. "Linguistic Areas in Europe: Their Boundaries and Political Significance." *Bulletin of the American Geographical Society* (47:6). Pg. 425.

6. Black Book. Pg. 23–24.

7. Black Book. Pg. 26.

8. Margaret MacMillan. 2001. *Paris 1919*. New York, Random House. Pg. 207.

9. Neil Smith. 2003. *American Empire: Roosevelt's Geographer and the Prelude to Globalization*. Berkeley: University of California Press. Pg. 150.

10. Isaiah Bowman. 1921. "Constantinople and the Balkans," in *What Really Happened at Paris: The Story of the Peace Conference, 1918–1919 by American Delegates*, ed. Edward House. New York: Charles Scribner's Sons. Pg. 162.

11. Commission on Polish Affairs Report No. 1, 03/12/1919. Miller Diary Document 498.

12. Ibid.

13. Isaiah Bowman. 1928. *The New World: Problems in Political Geography*. New York: World Book.

14. MacMillan, 2001. Pg. 218.

15. Notes of a Meeting Held at President Wilson's House in the Place des Etats-Unis, Paris, on Tuesday, April 22, 1919, at 11 a.m.: FRUS Vol. V. Pg. 114.

16. Preliminary Peace Conference Protocol #6, 05/06/1919: FRUS Vol. III. Pg. 344–345.

17. Treaty of Versailles, Articles 100–108.

18. MacMillan, 2001. Pg. 217.

19. Bowman, 1928. Pg. 412.

20. MacMillan, 2001. Pg. 219.

21. Bowman, 1928. Pg. 413.

22. Richard Hartshorne. 1933. "Geographic and Political Boundaries in Upper Silesia."*Annals of the Association of American Geographers* (23:4).

23. Howard Elcock. 1972. *Portrait of a Decision: The Council of Four and the Treaty of Versailles*. Birkenhead, UK: Eyre Methuen Ltd. Pg. 300; Lord, 1921.

24. Richard Hartshorne. 1937. "The Polish Corridor." *The Journal of Geography* (36:5).

25. Black Book. Pg. 24.

26. Ibid. Pg. 24–26.

27. Bowman, 1928. Pg. 432–435.

28. MacMillan, 2001. Pg. 225.

29. Black Book. Pg. 32–33.

30. For example, see Bowman, 1928 or Dominian, 1917.

31. Black Book. Pg. 24.

32. Bowman, 1928. Pg. 415–416.

33. Ibid. Pg. 329.

34. Ibid.

35. Seton-Watson, 1977.

36. Paul Mowrer. 1921. *Balkanized Europe: A Study in Political Analysis and Reconstruction*. New York: E.P. Dutton & Co.

37. David Stevenson. 2004. *Cataclysm: The First World War as Political Tragedy*. New York: Basic Books.

38. George White. 2000. *Nationalism and Territory: Constructing Group Identity in Southeastern Europe*. Lanham, MD: Rowman & Littlefield.

39. Bowman, 1928.

40. B.C. Wallis. 1918 (i). "The Peoples of Austria." *Geographical Review* (6:1).

41. Black Book. Pg. 40.

42. Ibid.

43. The Black Book. Pg. 40.

44. Black Book. Pg. 45–46.

45. MacMillan, 2001. Pg. 361–362.

46. Committee for the Study of Territorial Questions Relating to Rumania and Yugoslavia (CSTQ). *Report No. 2: Frontiers of Yugoslavia*. 4/19/1919.

47. MacMillan, 2001. Pg. 255.

48. Bowman, 1928. Pg. 311–313.

49. David Andelman. 2008. *A Shattered Peace: Versailles 1919 and the Price We Pay Today*. Hoboken, NJ: John Wiley & Sons. Pg. 212.

50. Charles Seymour. 1921. "The End of an Empire: Remnants of Austria-Hungary," in *What Really Happened at Paris: The Story of the Peace*

Conference, 1918–1919 by American Delegates, ed. Edward House. New York: Charles Scribner's Sons. Pg. 107.

51. Bowman, 1921; Mowrer, 1921.

52. Bowman, 1921. Pg. 170.

53. Arthur Link. 1965. "Wilson and the Liberal Peace Program," in Edwin Rozwenc and Thomas Lyons, *Realism and Idealism in Wilson's Peace Program*. Boston: DC Heath and Co.

54. Stevenson, 2004.

55. Leon Dominian. 1917. *Frontiers of Language and Nationality in Europe*. New York: Henry Holt and Company.

56. Jovan Cvijic. 1918. "The Geographical Distribution of the Balkan Peoples." *Geographical Review* (5:5).

57. Bowman, 1928.

58. Bullitt Lowry. 1996. *Armistice 1918*. Kent, OH: Kent State Press. Pg. 102.

59. Address of President Wilson to Congress, January 8, 1918.

60. Black Book. Pg. 41–42.

61. Minutes of the Daily Meetings of the Commissioners Plenipotentiary, Wednesday, March 12, 1919: FRUS Vol. XI, Pgs. 114–115.

62. Jeremy Crampton. 2006. "The Cartographic Calculation of Space: Race Mapping and the Balkans at the Paris Peace Conferece of 1919." *Social and Cultural Geography* (7:5).

63. Bowman, 1928.

64. Norman Hill. 1945. *Claims to Territory in International Law and Relations*. London: Oxford University.

65. Bowman, 1928.

66. Link, 1965.

67. Notes of a Meeting of the Big Four 4/19/1919: FRUS Vol. V, Pgs. 80–94.

68. Ibid.

69. Notes of a Meeting of the Big Four 4/19/1919: FRUS Vol. V, Pgs. 80–94.

70. Ibid.

71. Notes of a Meeting of the Big Four 4/20/1919: FRUS Vol. V, Pgs. 95–101.

72. MacMillan, 2001.

73. Notes of a Meeting of the Big Four (minus Italy) 4/22/1919: FRUS Vol. V, Pgs. 135–137.

74. Notes of a Meeting of the Big Four (minus Italy) 4/23/1919: FRUS Vol. V, Pgs. 149–151.

75. Notes of a Meeting of the Big Four (minus Italy) 5/13/1919: FRUS Vol. V, Pgs. 579–587.

76. Notes of a Meeting of the Big Four 5/28/1919: FRUS Vol. V, Pg. 80.

77. Notes of a Meeting of the Big Four 5/28/1919: FRUS Vol. V, Pgs. 90–91.

78. Letter from the Head of the Italian Delegation (Orlando) to the President of the Peace Conference (Clemenceau) 6/14/1919: FRUS Vol VI, Pgs. 485–486.

79. Douglas Johnson. 1921. "Fiume and the Adriatic Problem," in *What Really Happened at Paris: The Story of the Peace Conference, 1918–1919 by American Delegates*, ed. Edward House. New York: Charles Scribner's Sons. Pg. 139.

80. Mowrer, 1921. Pg. 238.

81. Bowman, 1928; Stevenson, 2004.

82. Bowman, 1928.

83. Richard Hartshorne. 1950. "The Functional Approach in Political Geography." *Annals of the Association of American Geographers* (40:2).

84. Seton-Watson, 1977. Pg. 109.

85. Black Book. Pg. 36.

86. Black Book. Pg. 36.

87. CSTQ. *Report No. 1: Rumanian Frontiers*. 4/9/1919. Pg. 5.

88. Ibid. Pg. 6.

89. Ibid. Pg. 17.

90. Note for the Supreme Council. Paris, May 24, 1919: FRUS Vol, VI. Pg. 591.

91. Bowman, 1928. Pg. 371–375.

CHAPTER 5

Negotiating Borders Part 3—
A Survey of Border Proposals
Not Adopted at the Conference

Although much of what the United States brought to the table in Paris came to fruition, several proposals failed to make it into the Paris treaties. Many parts of the American plan for peace were not adopted at the Paris Peace Conference, and in some cases not even considered by the Big Four. Past analysis and writing on the peace conference blames President Wilson for many of the perceived failings that took place in areas where the United States saw none of its proposals implemented, and in many cases places where the United States was not even included in the discussions over final arrangements.[1] A series of factors prevented parts of the Black Book plans from ever reaching the negotiations. These factors included a lack of time, quickly changing political situations in Eastern Europe, and the relatively small number of casualties suffered by the United States. These factors diminished leverage and strength at the negotiating table compared with Britain and France, who suffered the brunt of Allied casualties on the western front.

Many areas where the U.S. plan was not implemented, particularly those outside Europe, were placed nominally under the aegis of the League of Nations, with mandates given to the victorious powers, especially to Britain, France, Italy, and Japan. A mandate was a form of internationally administered colonialism, with a pledge that the region would eventually emerge as an independent state. Certain mandates, such as those in the Middle East, were supposed to be made fully independent within a short time frame, while mandates in Africa and the Pacific were not expected to be given such status in the foreseeable future, if ever.[2] Most mandates created in Paris would not gain independence during the period prior to World War II, although a small number would. The processes of post–World War II decolonization along with the breakup of the Soviet Union finally led to some of the American proposals in these regions coming closer to fruition, while many parts of the American plans in zones peripheral to the main negotiations at the Paris Peace Conference do not resemble anything close to today's political map. It is remarkable to see these plans in hindsight, especially to note the relevance many of them have to areas of major strife that continues to this day.

ALBANIA

Few European populations presented a greater conundrum for the great powers than the Albanians. As a tribal Muslim people who happened to reside in Europe, the Albanians seemed foreign and non-European. Attitudes of the time were prevalently racist and anti-Muslim, with favoritism shown to all other claimants in the Balkan region over those of the Albanians themselves. However, Albania had already emerged as an independent state in 1912, when European realms of the Ottoman Empire disintegrated during the Balkan Wars that directly predated the world war. In 1919, the Albanians wanted to maintain their status as an independent state and extend control to areas beyond their current borders, as large Albanian populations remained in other neighboring states, especially in Serbia (mainly in Kosovo and Macedonia) and in Montenegro.

During the war, the Italians claimed Albania as one of their war goals, as they wanted to gain the entire area as an Italian protectorate, granting Italy full control over the mouth of the Adriatic Sea. Despite Albania's status as a neutral state, Italy invaded Albania during the war, and in 1914 it took control of Valona (now known as Vlorë), a port city in southern Albania, with the aim of holding the territory after the war.[3] Italy had been promised this port in the secret Treaty of London concluded with Britain and France. By war's end, not only did Italy control parts of the south and center of the country, but the rest of Albania endured either Serb or Greek occupation.

Unlike Italy, the United States remained committed to an independent Albania as part of the new world order. This position stood despite the attitude of Americans toward Albanians at the time. Writing in the *Geographical Review*, geographer Charles Woods described

Albanians as, "a warlike, lawless people, but nevertheless they have their own—and a very strict—code of honor and they are faithful even unto death."[4] Woods noted the Albanian situation would be complex, with competing claims from Italy, Serbia and Greece over parts of its territory. Despite calls for Albania to remain independent, it was widely accepted that Albania would need some sort of mandate to aid in overseeing its affairs, at least for the short term.[5] The call for even a mandate in a place that had already been self-governing demonstrates the bias against Albanians held widely at the time.

The American peace planners realized that Albania would pose an especially complex problem, one which the Black Book addresses without presenting a particularly hard and fast proposal for the United States to recommend as how to best rectify the Albanian situation (see Figure 5.1). Although presenting many options, the American plan endorsed as the best a mandate without extending the borders of Albania beyond prewar limits. The plan did, however, call for Greece to gain areas in the south that were primarily populated by Greeks, and for Italy to maintain a mandate over Valona.[6] Clearly, the Inquiry had in mind a minimalist view as to the future disposition of Albania. Rather than proposing that all of the Muslim Albanian populations be consolidated into a state, the American plan called for the reduction of Albania to an even smaller unit than that which emerged from the Balkan Wars, a plan that seems to run counter to Wilsonian principles, and one clearly informed by the anti-Muslim sentiment of most academics and politicians of the time.

At the peace conference, the Commission on Greek and Albanian Affairs was created to handle all claims in southern Albania, while the northern border was settled as part of the creation of Yugoslavia (see chapter 4). Britain and France strongly supported Greece's claims to southern Albania, while Italy claimed the entire region, and the United States maintained a distanced position.[7] Horse trading commenced among the powers while excluding the United States. The Albanians desperately reached out in any direction they could for assistance.

In the Council of Four, discussions of Albania arose irregularly, and a final arrangement was never agreed to at the Paris Peace Conference. The Albanian turmoil continued into the 1920s, with Yugoslavia, Italy and Greece staking claims over parts of the country while internal political disorder raged.[8] Albania survived, and expelled outside forces

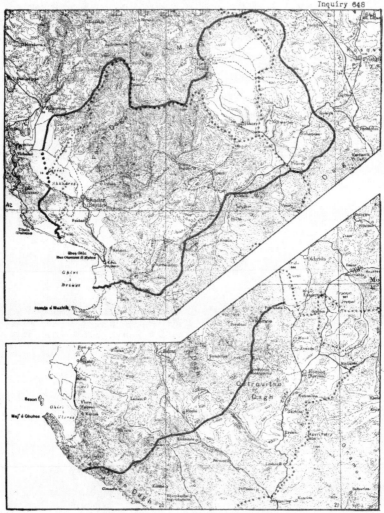

Figure 5.1. *Black Book Map of Albania: Rather than defining proposed borders for Albania, the Black Book only lays out a proposed area in the north for a Yugoslav protectorate and a proposed new southern border with Greece to the north of the border drawn at the end of the Balkan Wars. The area Italy was to maintain control over around Valona was not defined by the Inquiry, nor was the final border for the proposed mandate state of Albania. (Map from JHU Bowman Papers MS 58 13.13)*

from all areas except around Vlorë, which the Italians maintained control of during the interwar period. Albania finally fell to Italy at the start of World War II, but emerged from the war in control of all formerly Italian areas. The borders set at the end of World War II remain Albania's borders today.

THE AEGEAN ISLANDS

At war's end, Italy maintained occupation forces in control of a series of Aegean islands that it captured in 1912, formerly under Turkish control, including Rhodes and the nearby Dodecanese islands, just off the Turkish coast. Italy wished to retain control of these islands, despite their Greek populations, as Italy's war aims included gaining a foothold in the eastern Mediterranean. Just as in the Tyrol and parts of Albania, the Dodecanese were promised to Italy as part of the secret Treaty of London.

The American plan for peace called for the transfer of the Greek populated islands of the Aegean to Greece:

> It is recommended that Rhodes and the Dodecanese be assigned to Greece.
>
> Over 80% of the population of Rhodes and the Dodecanese are Greek Orthodox. They are bitterly opposed to the present Italian occupation, and should be assigned to the mother country.[9]

Over 100,000 Greeks and fewer than 12,000 other people resided in these islands at war's end.[10] Based on Wilsonian ideals, these islands were rightfully part of Greece and not Italy. The disposition of these small islands would prove to be yet another exceptionally difficult issue, pitting two Allied states against each other in territorial claims, with the Italians as a member of the Big Four holding a strong upper hand over the Greeks.

Control of the Dodecanese was but one of many areas where the Italians disrupted the peace conference. After walking out over the Istrian region (see chapter 4), Italy returned to the conference and over the summer considered ceding Greece control of the Dodecanese, as long as Italy could retain the principal island of Rhodes.[11] The Greeks would hear none of it, and the final status of the islands remained unclear at the end of the Paris Peace Conference. In the Treaty of Lausanne, the final peace treaty with Turkey only signed in 1923, Italy was granted these islands. Not until Italy's defeat in World War II were the islands finally ceded to Greece. Although it was several decades late in coming, the American proposal for these islands has now become the lasting international agreement, with the Greeks exercising sovereignty over these overwhelmingly Greek-inhabited islands.

UKRAINE

When the 1918 armistice agreements ended the fighting, the Russian Empire had devolved into total chaos. Planning how to dispose of the Russian territories in the midst of the Bolshevik Revolution was exceedingly complicated. The Baltic States and Finland emerged from the peace conference, much as envisioned by the Inquiry (see chapter 4). However, others would not come into existence, or at least not remain on the world map for long during the chaos that enveloped the postwar period. In the throes of the Russian Revolution, a Ukrainian state was declared in 1918. Due to the instability and conflict that permeated the region, a series of provisional states would develop over the coming few years, but none were to last more than a few months before other entities replaced them.

The American Inquiry was concerned about the viability of a separate Ukrainian state. Scholars of the time often referred to Ukrainians as "little Russians," and were unsure as to whether they were indeed a separate nationality from Russians. Scholarship pointed to differences between Ukrainians and Russians, but whether these were enough to deem them a separate people was unclear.[12] Rather than proposing a permanent independent state, the Black Book proposal for Ukraine called for a temporary state that would eventually vote on whether to join with Russia or remain independent (see Figure 5.2):

> It is recommended: That encouragement be given, at opportune times, to the reunion with Russia of those border regions to the south and west which have broken away and set up their own national governments...

Figure 5.2.   Black Book Map of Western Russia: Along with Finland, Poland and the three Baltic States, the Inquiry proposed a provisional Ukrainian state. The western regions of this state (which had been the province of Galicia in Austria) were to go to Ukraine, if created, and otherwise given to Poland. (Map from JHU Bowman Papers MS 58 13.13)

It is recommended that there be established a Ukrainian state, provided Ukrainian nationalism is strong enough to justify that decision.

The Ukraine today is in a state of chaos, and it is still uncertain which will gain the upper hand, the Russian sympathies of the upper classes or the Bolshevist or anarchist tendencies of the masses.[13]

The Black Book also proposed that the region of Galicia—formerly part of Austria, which was eventually joined to Poland, should be given to Ukraine if possible:

If at the time of decision by the peace conference the Ukraine should give evidences of vitality, the disputed belt should be assigned to it, because in that region the Ukrainians (although very backward in culture) outnumber the Poles two to one.[14]

What exactly was meant by "strong enough" nationalism remains unclear in the American plans or literature. This area had significant differences from greater Russia, enough that the Ukrainian Rada (Parliament) had attempted to separate their territory from Russia on several occasions. It is noteworthy that if Ukrainian nationalism seemed strong enough, a separate state would emerge including not just Ukrainian areas, but also the Crimean Peninsula, which was inhabited mostly by Russians and Crimean Tatars. Areas of Austria-Hungary with Ukrainian populations were set aside for the Ukrainians, if they chose statehood, but would be granted to Poland otherwise, and not to Russia.

These sorts of arrangements make it difficult to accurately interpret the logic behind the Inquiry's thinking. If Ukrainians did exhibit strong enough nationalism, would it not be more sensible to at least place all Ukrainians in one state based on self-determination principles, whether that be Russia or Poland? It is interesting, as well, that the Inquiry proposed the inclusion of the Crimean Peninsula in Ukraine, as this region clearly did not fit into a Ukrainian state based on the concept of self-determination, and to this day remains a difficult region for Ukraine to control, due to population differences and other factors.

Dealing with Ukraine, much like the other Russian parts of the settlement was greatly complicated by the lack of Russian representation at the conference and the fluid political situation in the Russian imperial lands. Events overtook discussion on what to do about Ukraine, and discussions in the Big Four ended up centering on how to counter the

Bolshevik threat in Ukraine, rather than on creating an independent state or any other political disposition of the territory.[15]

The Soviet Russian state that emerged from the revolution was not the democratic or even federal state that the American Inquiry called for in their original plans. However, the Red Army preempted a lasting Ukrainian independence with their invasion in 1919. Distracted by other issues further west, the peace conference failed to make any final decision regarding this hapless area. The Soviets made Ukraine nominally autonomous as a separate republic in the USSR, one that would even be granted a separate seat in the United Nations post–World War II. It would not be until 1991 that a truly independent Ukrainian state would emerge. Although not exactly on the same lines as those envisioned by the Inquiry, Ukraine today does retain the Crimea and the regions that the Inquiry recommended be given to Ukraine, rather than Poland.

RUTHENIA

Although Ukraine would emerge as an independent state long after the Paris Peace Conference, a neighboring area addressed by the Inquiry, Ruthenia, now lies within Ukraine, but has never enjoyed a truly separate independent status. What is even meant by the term Ruthenia is subject to debate. At the time, most people understood Ruthenian to mean a Catholic Ukrainian, versus the majority Orthodox Ukrainians who lived further to the east. Should this area be part of Ukraine, Poland, Czechoslovakia or Romania? That was the principal question of the day.

The tiny region of Ruthenia was set aside for consideration by the Inquiry. This area was administered as proposed by the Inquiry, but only for a short time, as it found itself annexed by the Soviet Union by 1945. The preferred option for the Ruthenes was followed in the final settlements, but the Black Book contained two options to deal with this small region to provide more latitude for the American negotiators. The first option was for Ruthenia to be administered as a League of Nations mandate by Czechoslovakia, and the second option was to incorporate Ruthenia directly into that same state.[16]

The option of creating a mandate for Ruthenia was not widely discussed in Paris and never made it into discussions by the Big Four. Rather, only debate over what should be given to the Czechs versus the Romanians made it into high-level discussions. In the Treaty of St. Germain (the Austrian treaty), Czechoslovakia was granted Ruthenia with the proviso that it be set aside as an autonomous region within the state.[17] The area would go on to play only a minor role in the Czechoslovak state, due to its small economy and low level of development.[18] Only 460,000 people resided in this small territory at the time.[19] In the opening days of World War II, Ruthenia declared independence on March 15, 1939. It lasted one day. The Red Army quickly overran and integrated Ruthenia into the Ukrainian Soviet Socialist Republic following the war. Today it remains part of Ukraine as the Transcarpathian region, or Zakarpattia, the only part of Ukraine to extend over the Carpathian Mountains into the Hungarian Plains to the west.

TRANSCAUCASIA—GEORGIA & AZERBAIJAN

Just as did Ukraine, Georgia and Azerbaijan temporarily gained independence during the Russian Revolution. They formed a short-lived Transcaucasian republic under the constantly shifting political situation throughout the lands of the former Russian Empire. The area then divided into multiple states: Georgia, Azerbaijan and Armenia (which will be discussed later in this chapter). By the start of the Paris Peace Conference, these regions functioned as quasi-independent separate states.

The Inquiry considered this region in the plans they submitted for use in Paris. Rather than outright granting of independence, provisional status was all the Inquiry felt either Georgia or Azerbaijan could handle (see Figures 5.2 and 5.3). For Georgia:

> It is recommended that the Georgians receive provisional independence.
>
> The proposed state of Georgia would have an ample outlet upon the Black Sea... would have an excellent northern frontier in the snowy heights of the Caucuses Mountains, would be limited on the east by a fairly clear-cut ethnic line, and on the south by the borders of the Armenian highlands....
>
> Possibly the Georgians would wish to join Armenia in some federal scheme, and if this could be accomplished it might well be to their mutual advantage. There have developed between them a certain amount of political difference, and for this reason a provisional independence is recommended. If his tension can be diminished a future union would be desirable.[20]

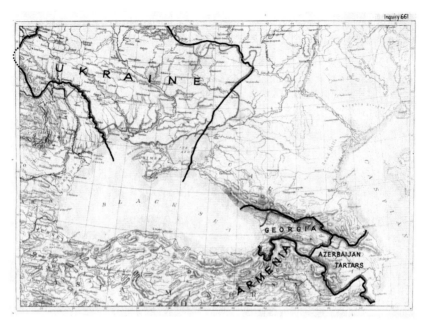

Figure 5.3. *Black Book Map of Ukraine and the Caucuses: The Black Book provided for the creation of several new states in southern Russia. In Transcaucasia, the Inquiry proposed the creation of Georgia, Azerbaijan and a large Armenian state that would extend all the way into eastern Turkey. (Map from JHU Bowman Papers MS 58 13.13)*

Similarly, the Azeris were to be given a provisional status:

It is recommended that the Azerbaijan Tatars receive provisional independence.

The Azerbaijan Tatars are a distinct ethnic group requiring separate consideration on account of marked differences of race and religion. Were this group to be included in a Georgian or Armenian state it would constitute a disturbing element. Hence provisional independence is recommended, pending the stabilizing of the states in the region, and a possible union with Georgia and Armenia.[21]

Clearly any sort of Transcaucasian union, such as the one that existed temporarily from 1918–1919, was not favored by the Inquiry, based on the difference between Christian Georgians and Armenians, and the Muslim Azeris. However, the "clear-cut ethnic line" discussed in the Black Book was not as tidy as the Inquiry presented it. Providing for self-determination in the South Caucuses was no easy feat with overlapping homelands for all three ethnic groups in the region.[22] These plans also failed to account for other ethnic groups in the area including Ossetians, Chechens, Abkhazians, and many others.

Events in the region, rather than decisions at the Paris Peace Conference, determined the outcome for the Georgians and Azeris. Although their forces were able to hold off the White (imperial) Russian army, by 1921 the Red Army moved southward and integrated Transcaucasia into the USSR. After a brief stint with independence between 1918–1921, these states would finally reemerge with the breakup of the Soviet Union in 1991, although with borders drawn by the USSR under Josef Stalin rather than those proposed at the Paris Peace Conference.

BREAKING UP CENTRAL TURKEY— GREATER ARMENIA & THE STRAITS

Unlike the Georgians and Azeris, for which the western powers manifested only limited interest, there was strong support for the creation of an independent Armenia, and one that would have been much larger than the Armenian state that emerged from the remnants of the Soviet Union in 1991. The situation for the Armenians was dire throughout the war. With the upheaval in the Ottoman Empire and the Turkish nationalist revolution, the first major genocide of the 20th century erupted in Turkey, consisting of a series of deportations and mass executions that began under the Ottomans and were continued by the Young Turks after the Ottoman collapse. At the peace conference, memory of the recent events was fresh and shocking to the leaders of the Great Powers. These events greatly influenced Wilson's position regarding Armenia and his strong advocacy on behalf of the Armenian claims being made in Paris.

As in many of the Balkan settlements, the specter of secret treaties would come to haunt the settlements in Turkey. The Treaty of Saint Jean de Maurienne divided up spheres of influence in Ottoman lands among Britain, France and Italy.[23] The non-Turkish regions were to be divvied up, while a rump Turkey would be left in Anatolia.[24] More importantly, the Sykes-Picot Agreement between Britain and France split colonial claims within the Middle East between these two powers and would have tremendous influence on the final disposition of Middle Eastern territory. Not only was the United States not party to these agreements, it never declared war on Ottoman Turkey and maintained diplomatic relations throughout the conflict. Despite this, the United States made extensive plans on how to deal with the lands of the Ottoman Empire after the war, as it was clear they would be considered at the conference.

More than any other part of the Middle East settlements, it was expected that action would take place regarding Armenia. American delegate William Westermann noted after the conference, but prior to Soviet annexation, "The liberation of Armenia was the one outstanding result expected from the Near Eastern negotiations at the Peace Conference."[25] President Wilson hinted at such, without explicitly promising it, in the twelfth his Fourteen Points:

> The Turkish portion of the present Ottoman Empire should be assured a secure sovereignty, but the other nationalities which are now under Turkish rule should be assured an undoubted security of life and an absolutely unmolested opportunity of autonomous development, and the Dardanelles should be permanently opened as a free passage to the ships and commerce of all nations under international guarantees.[26]

This guidance from the President did not clearly promise anything beyond autonomy for the subject peoples of Turkey, but in the final proposals that Wilson's experts would prepare, total division from Turkey would be proposed for a series of peoples including Armenians and Arabs. The Inquiry would also prepare a proposal for the Bosphorus and Dardanelles Straits, to ensure that these key connectors between the Mediterranean and Black Seas remain open for international use.

The Black Book proposed a major new Armenian state under a League of Nations mandate (see Figure 5.4):

> It is recommended that the Armenians of Transcaucasia be given permanent independence as part of the new Armenian state.
>
> The Armenians of Transcaucasia form a compact group of people near the historic homeland of the Armenoid race. Though they were under the Russian flag in 1914 they represent one of the peripheral groups absorbed in relatively late years by the slowly expanding empire of the Czars. No local differences set them apart from their kinsmen in Turkey, and they should be reunited with the rest of the Armenian population in that region in order 1) to give the new state every reasonable element of strength; 2) to follow the principle of grouping in a common domain people of like religion, political sympathies and speech.[27]

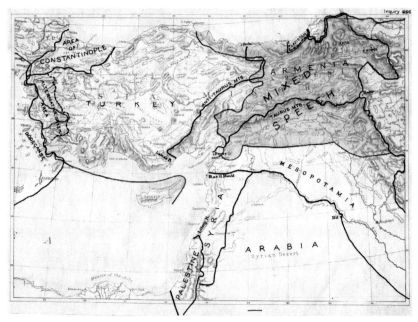

Figure 5.4. Black Book Map of Turkey, Armenia & the Levant: The Inquiry proposed the creation of a greatly reduced Turkey on the Anatolian Peninsula. In far western Anatolia, it was proposed that Greece may take certain areas. To the east, a very large Armenian state was proposed that runs through not only Armenian areas, but also large areas where the Kurds and Turks made up a large portion of the population, all the way to the coast of the Mediterranean Sea. Further south, three new mandates were proposed—Mesopotamia, Syria and Palestine. (Map from JHU Bowman Papers MS 58 13.13)

The Armenian issue was complex, and the Inquiry anticipated the U.S. negotiators, especially the President, would need extensive background to move forward on negotiations to create this new Armenian state. The Black Book recognized the Armenians in Russia had already broken free, but that they should be combined in a state with the Armenians of Turkey, as well. It is also noteworthy that because of the genocide and long-running political problems for the Armenian people, the Inquiry felt that the new Armenian state should also include vast areas where Armenians were either a plurality, or even a minority, especially in Kurdish regions of the former Ottoman Empire.

Discussions at the Paris Peace Conference on the disposition of Turkish territories were ongoing among the Big Four. It was agreed that northern Turkey would be set aside for a mandate under the League of Nations. The Treaty of Sevres called for an independent

Armenia, but did not specify its borders.[28] The United States was asked in this treaty to take on the responsibility to govern the Armenian mandate, but events in the region preempted any American action.[29] Furthermore, the failure of the U.S. to join the League of Nations precluded the United States from taking on any mandates. No state stepped forward to assume the Armenian mandate after the peace conference.[30] The United States had been proposed as the mandatory power for Armenia, because of President Wilson's personal interest in the Armenian cause. It was clear in the United States that this was not to be, as there was no interest in the United States Senate to take on the mandate.[31] The Armenian territories once part of Russia ended up becoming part of the Soviet Union in 1921 following the Red Army's invasion, while the remaining regions proposed for Armenia were integrated into the new Turkish state and recognized as such by the Treaty of Lausanne, signed in 1923. The modern Armenian state occupies only those areas under Soviet control in the 1920s, and did not reemerge as an independent state until 1991.

The dismantling of Turkey involved not only a proposed Greater Armenia, but also the creation of a new internationalized zone along the strategic Bosphorus and Dardanelles Straits connecting the Mediterranean and Black Seas. This would have resulted in Turkey losing Istanbul (referred to in American documents of the time as Constantinople), the largest Turkish-speaking city in the world, to a new internationalized territory. The American plan called for (see Figure 5.5):

1. That there be established in the Constantinople region an internationalized state.
2. That the new state be given such a governmental organization by the appointment of a power as a mandatory of the League of Nations or otherwise, as may seem most expedient to the peace conference....
4. That the Bosphorus, Sea of Marmora, and Dardanelles be permanently opened as a free passageway to the ships and commerce of all nations, under international guarantees.[32]

Wilson's twelfth point specifically indicated an internationalization of the Zone of the Straits. This also related back to Wilson's call in the second of the Fourteen Points for freedom of the seas. As many proposed and current states (Romania, Bulgaria, Ukraine, Russia and

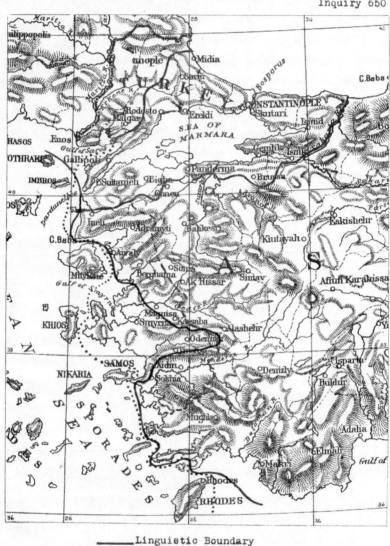

_____Linguistic Boundary

Figure 5.5.   *Black Book Map of the Straits and Greek Areas of Turkey: The Black Book proposed the creation of an international zone around the Bosphorus and Dardanelles, connecting the Black Sea with the Mediterranean Sea. It was also suggested that Greece may take control of the Greek populated areas around Smyrna, on the Turkish coastal region of Ionia. (Map from JHU Bowman Papers MS 58 13.13)*

Georgia) needed access to the high seas through the Bosphorus, it was felt that only bringing this area under international control could guarantee such an arrangement over the long term.

The Zone of the Straits was proposed in the Treaty of Sevres of 1920. However, rather than extending Bulgarian territory into the areas north of Istanbul as the Inquiry envisioned, it was proposed that Greece take these Turkish-inhabited areas. Due to the civil war raging within Turkey, this never took place. The subsequent 1923 Treaty of Lausanne ceded these areas to Turkey, and today the entire region remains under Turkish control, but open to international shipping.

Along with the creation of these two states, the Inquiry recommended the creation of a Turkish state, one much smaller than that which would emerge in the years following the peace conference. The American proposal for Turkey allowed for the creation of a League of Nations mandate over a state located entirely on the Anatolian Peninsula, and one that included the region of Smyrna (now known as Izmir), whose occupation led to grave consequences for the Greeks:

> An outstanding feature is the presence, in Asia Minor, west of the Anti-Taurus Mountains, of a solid block of Turkish Moslems. They constitute a sound Anatolian peasantry whose chance of independent development deserves every consideration. The fact is patent, and with fresh opportunities of development the proposed state may in time have both stability and power. Not the least of its assets would be freedom from the burden of governing alien peoples of different faith, whose oppression by the Turk has reacted upon him morally and politically, with well-known evil effects....
>
> Although an alternative Greek area is shown in the Smyrna region, it is not part of this recommendation that it be assigned to Greece. The arguments for such assignment have been scrutinized with great care, and it is felt to be unsafe from every standpoint, commercial, strategic, and political, to give Greece a foothold upon the mainland of Asia Minor. The possession of the Dodecanese puts Greek people, Greek ships and Greek merchants, at the very doors of the new state. To give her a foothold upon the mainland would be to invite immediate trouble. Greece would press her claims for more territory; Turkey would feel that her new boundaries were run so as to give her a great handicap at the very start. The harbor of Smyrna has been for centuries an outlet for the products of the central Anatolian valleys and upland.[33]

The Inquiry foresaw the problems of a Greek presence on the mainland of Turkey in an area that would soon lead to a Greek disaster.

As in other parts of the Turkish settlement, the Americans held very little sway regarding the disposition of these territories. The United States was the only state at the conference to fully oppose the Greek claim to the territory around Smyrna.[34] Britain and France supported Greek claims, but only pushed for a small territory surrounding the majority Greek-populated city of Smyrna.[35] Smyrna was the most populous city in the Greek-speaking world at the time, with around 375,000 people.[36] Despite this, the hinterlands of the city were overwhelmingly Turkish in population. Greece gained Smyrna in the Treaty of Sevres. In 1922, Mustafa Kemal's army invaded, captured the city and expelled the entire Greek population. All that remains today to remind us of the Greek impact on the Smyrna region are the countless Ancient Greek ruins that dot this picturesque coast.

The Turkish treaty manifested bits of the American peace plan, but clearly did not follow what the Inquiry had in mind for the disposition of Turkey in any major way. The lack of an American declaration of war on Turkey and the departure of the U.S. plenipotentiaries from Paris before the completion of the Treaty of Sevres are the principal reasons the American plan for this region was not adopted. Instead, the secret agreements made by other Allied states took precedence and led to many years of continued instability on the periphery of modern Turkey.

MESOPOTAMIA, THE LEVANT & PALESTINE

Further south, within the lands of the Ottoman Empire, a series of mandate colonies would emerge from the Paris Peace Conference. Although supposedly temporary, many of these would persist until the era of decolonization led to the emergence of the modern Middle Eastern states, along lines very similar to those set out at the Paris Peace Conference and in meetings just following. Unlike in Europe, where language was viewed as the principle criterion for self-determination, it was religion that was selected in the Middle East as the key indicator to divide different groups of people.[37]

The Americans supported the call for a series of mandates throughout the Middle East, including a mandate in Mesopotamia, although one quite different than the British mandate formed in Iraq after the war. The Black Book called for this new state:

> The Mesopotamian area... is a racial unit. There is an Arab linguistic unity south of a line drawn from Alexandretta to the Persian border. Above this line live Arabs, Armenians, Turks, Kurds and Assyrians, each group speaking a distinct language. Below this line there is comparatively a much higher degree of unity. It is essential to the development of the great irrigation projects below Baghdad that the headwaters of the Tigris River, and as much of the Euphrates as possible, should be under a single administration. The welfare of the foothills of Kurdistan and of the great steppe region of Mesopotamia is bound up with the irrigable lowlands of the Tigris and Euphrates basin....
>
> The southern border of the area lies at the edge of the Arabian desert, where new relationships come in and different political treatment....
>
> Nothing should be done to preclude the possibility of the future development of an Arab confederation, including Mesopotamia, as an alternate solution which would be desirable.[38]

Despite the large population mix, the United States did go forward with a single Mesopotamian state. However, as can be seen in the map (Figure 5.4), the proposed state is quite different in borders from the Iraqi mandate that would emerge from Paris and remains on the map as Iraq today. Although Kurdish and Shiite Arab areas were included, most of the Sunni parts of modern Iraq are included in a separate Arabian state to the south. Also, most of what became Syria after the war was included in this Mesopotamian state, thereby eliminating the divide between these two Arab countries that share similar culture and religion. The state that would emerge had "extremely artificial frontiers," due to the mixture of ethnic and religious groups placed into the state.[39]

This proposal largely ignores the Kurds. In the American plan, they would have been divided between Armenia and Mesopotamia (and the Kurdish areas of Iran remain inside Persia under the American plan, as well). Following the settlements, the Kurds were placed into four states (Turkey, Syria, Persia and Iraq), versus only two (Persia and the Ottoman Empire) prior to World War I. This created what would become one of the most difficult and long-standing territory-boundary-identity issues in the world, one that today holds the Kurds as one of the most populous national groups anywhere to not have their own state.[40]

The American plan for the Levantine region (the Middle Eastern coastal areas along the Mediterranean) stood out as remarkably different from the final mandates created at the conference. While much of what became Syria and Transjordan were included in the Mesopotamian state called for by the United States, two smaller states along the coast were championed by the Americans—Syria and Palestine. The Syrian state recommended by the Americans resembles modern Lebanon much more so than modern Syria, although it includes areas now inside both of those states and modern Jordan. The Syrian state was proposed as a mandate in the Black Book that would eventually form a state for the Christian and Muslim populations of the coastal parts of the Levant (see Figure 5.4):

> While Syria belongs to the Arab-speaking world, it has an unusually large European population, close commercial and cultural relations with Europe, a strong Christian element, and a sedentary mode of life. It should therefore be separated at the outset from the nomad Arab area.[41]

The exact boundaries of the American proposed Syria differ from what France drew for Lebanon after the war, but in principle, this would be a similar state to the one that did emerge as a mandate for France.

Most notably, the American plan proposed a Jewish state in Palestine, initially under a British mandate. The plan for Palestine acknowledged the complexities inherent in the creation of such a state, and the immense difficulties that such a state would face in governing the Holy Land. The Black Book provides minute detail regarding how Palestine was to be set up and eventually developed into a Jewish state:

> It is recommended that there be established a separate state of Palestine.
>
> The separation of the Palestinian area from Syria finds justification in the religious experience of mankind. The Jewish and Christian churches were born in Palestine, and Jerusalem was for long years, at different periods, the capital of each. And while the relation of the Mohammedans to Palestine is not so intimate, from beginning they have regarded Jerusalem as a holy place. Only by establishing Palestine as a separate state can justice be done to these great facts....
>
> Palestine would obviously need wise and firm guidance. Its population is without political experience, is racially composite, and could easily become distracted by fanaticism and bitter religious differences....

It is recommended that the Jews be invited to return to Palestine and settle there, being assured by the Conference of all proper assistance in so doing that may be consistent with the protection of the personal (especially the religious) and the property rights of the non-Jewish population, and being further assured that it will be the policy of the League of Nations to recognize Palestine as a Jewish state as soon as it is a Jewish state in fact....

It was the cradle and home of their vital race, which has made large spiritual contributions to mankind, and is the only land in which they can hope to find a home of their own; they being in this last respect unique among significant peoples.

At present, however, the Jews form barely a sixth of the total population of 700,000 in Palestine, and whether they are to form a majority, or even a plurality, of the population in the future state remains uncertain. Palestine, in short, is far from being a Jewish country now. England, as mandatory, can be relied on to give the Jews the privileged position they should have without sacrificing the rights of non-Jews....

It is recommended that the holy places and religious rights of all creeds in Palestine be placed under the protection of the League of Nations and its mandatory. The basis for this recommendation is self-evident.[42]

The Americans, along with the other Allied powers, accepted the Balfour Declaration, calling for the creation of a Jewish homeland in Palestine.[43] American support was partially gained through lobbying by Jewish groups in the United States that supported self-determination for their kin.[44] Though there was not a Jewish majority, nor anything near it yet, the future course of events dramatically shaped Jewish fortunes in the region, and the Inquiry position stands in clear support of massive Jewish immigration into the region, which once it took place, has made enormous impacts on the political landscape of the Middle East.

At the peace conference, those supporting Zionism managed only one audience with the major powers. The difficulties of dealing with the German, Austrian and Hungarian treaties were so great that the Big Four were preoccupied with other matters and did not spend much time or effort considering the Zionist or anti-Zionist cases.

These distractions, compounded by the United States' lack of influence over Ottoman matters led to the disposition of the entire northern Middle East without significant American influence. President Wilson had wanted an end to secret agreements, such as Sykes-Picot, but the

French-British partitions of the region went forward. The mandates were assigned and borders drawn between them at the San Remo Conference on April 26, 1920, in a manner that did anything but stabilize the volatile situation in the region.[45] The United States was notably absent from the San Remo Conference and had no involvement in the disposition of these territories. Only Britain, France, Italy and Japan participated.

Despite the lack of American involvement, much of the blame assigned today is heaped upon the United States for the disposition of the Middle Eastern settlements. Many historical examples go so far as to place blame on the drawing of the map of the modern Middle East to Isaiah Bowman, America's chief geographer at the conference.[46] Clearly, from both the Black Book maps and the lack of American inclusion in the Middle Eastern discussions, President Wilson and his experts cannot take the blame for the resulting map and arrangements in this area. If anything, the United States was the Great Power with the least responsibility for the Middle Eastern borders drawn in 1920.

The borders crafted at the San Remo Conference have persisted in the Middle East except in the case of Israel, although the constituent territories created in San Remo—Iraq, Syria, Lebanon, Palestine and Transjordan—no longer are under European mandatory control. Blame can be assessed for the instability of every one of these states in part because the borders do not reflect demographic reality. Mixed populations in Lebanon, Iraq, Jordan, Israel and the Occupied Palestinian Territories have led to the political problems seen in the region to this day. These impacts make the final arrangements from the Paris Peace Conference relevant to the situation in the region as it currently stands. One can only wonder at the possibilities if the American border proposals had been adopted, although it is likely that these would not have brought full stability to the region.

ARABIA

Few locations confounded the American experts as much as the Arabian Peninsula, a region where the British maintained a significant presence on the coastal fringe, but where the desert interior remained an unbounded series of territories under the control of different Arab tribal kingdoms and clans. As such, it was difficult to propose any concrete plans for the area, and there was strong advocacy to allow political developments, beyond the British zone, to move forward without strong international involvement. The Black Book laid out some basic guidelines for the Arabian region, but did not make explicit recommendations as to the future demarcation of borders in this area (see Figure 5.6):

> It is recommended that the desert portion of the Arabian peninsula, exclusive of the agricultural areas of Syria and of the Euphrates and Tigris valleys, be treated as a separate block.

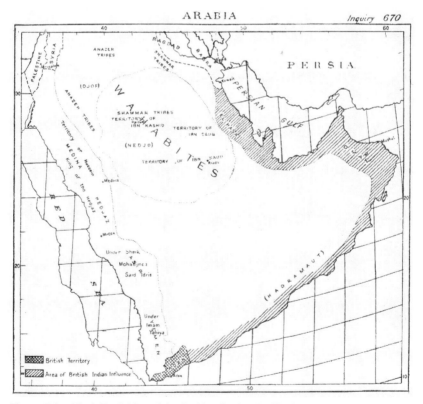

Figure 5.6. Black Book Map of the Arabian Peninsula: The Inquiry supported the continued British control and influence over the littoral regions of Arabia. However, for the interior, they recommended that political events be able to take their own course, rather than imposing a specific settlement on the region. (Map from JHU Bowman Papers MS 58 13.13)

In regard to this large desert area of Arabia, it is unwise to take decisive action at present....

The chieftains of the inner desert tribes, especially Ibn Saud, are absolutely opposed to the extension on the part of the king of Hedjaz. The sheikhs of Asir and Yemen would look with equal hostility on the consolidation of his power....

It is recommended that the policing of the Red Sea, Indian Ocean, and Persian Gulf Coasts of Arabia, and the border lands behind these, be left to the British Empire.[47]

The Americans proposal, in many ways, resembles what took place in this region following the peace conference. Only in the delimitation of the northern bounds of the Arabian area is it different, as parts of modern Jordan and Iraq that are majority Sunni are also included with their co-religionists to the south in the American plan.

Those wishing to influence the decisions made regarding Arabia have gone down as some of the most colorful and famous people to visit the peace conference, including T.E. Lawrence, better known as "Lawrence of Arabia," and Feisal, the Hashemite king (the Hashemite family would go on to rule both Iraq and Jordan later in the 20th century). Although audiences were granted with the Big Four, no decisions were made until the San Remo Conference of 1920. San Remo did not address areas south of the mandates, and it was left, as the Inquiry had suggested, to the Arab tribes to solve what would happen in the Arabian Peninsula.

Over the coming years, the tribes of Ibn Saud overran the Kingdom of the Hedjaz, gaining control of Mecca and Medina. In 1932, the Kingdom of Saudi Arabia was declared. Only with decolonization did the other states of the Arabian Peninsula emerge from British control, and the desert frontiers were not all settled with exact borders by the end of the 20th century. Despite European political intrigue and machinations in the region, the fate of Arabia hued more closely to what the United States proposed in Paris than either the British or French probably wanted, but it was not American efforts that led to this course of events.

CONCLUSION

In many areas on the eastern fringe of regions negotiated in Paris, the Americans came with plans only to find themselves sidelined. A combination of factors, mostly outside American control, led to these settlements being handled without much American involvement. However, what these proposals do show is that the United States had made painstaking plans, based mostly on the principles of Woodrow Wilson, to deal with the territorial settlements of Eastern Europe and the Middle East. In many ways, the Inquiry plans have been vindicated in Eastern Europe, as borders similar to the ones they proposed have come into existence for Ukraine and the Caucuses. In the Middle Eastern case, most of the borders of 1920 have persisted, but not due to their reflection of the self-determination of the people therein. Certainly it is difficult to make any solid argument that the borders of Iraq, Lebanon, Syria or Israel accurately reflect the ethnic, cultural or religious divides that characterize the region then or now. It is impossible to know if the American plan would have created a more stable Middle East than the current one, but it is highly unlikely that the imposition of the American plan would have led to a less stable environment than that which currently characterizes this volatile region.

NOTES

1. For example, see: David Andelman. 2008. *A Shattered Peace: Versailles 1919 and the Price We Pay Today*. Hoboken, NJ: John Wiley & Sons.

2. Manley Hudson. 1921. "The Protection of Minorities and Natives in Transferred Territories," in *What Really Happened at Paris: The Story of the Peace Conference, 1918–1919 by American Delegates*, ed. Edward House. New York: Charles Scribner's Sons. Pg. 225–226.

3. H. Charles Woods. 1918. "Albania and the Albanians." *Geographical Review* (5:4).

4. Ibid. Pg. 263.

5. Ibid. Pg. 273; George Scriven. 1919. "The Awakening of Albania." *Geographical Review* (8:2). Pg. 83.

6. Black Book. Pg. 57–58.

7. Margaret MacMillan. 2001. *Paris 1919*. New York, Random House. Pg. 356–357.

8. Isaiah Bowman. 1921. "Constantinople and the Balkans," in *What Really Happened at Paris: The Story of the Peace Conference, 1918–1919 by American Delegates*, ed. Edward House. New York: Charles Scribner's Sons. Pg. 174.

9. Black Book. Pg. 61.

10. Bowman, 1928. Pg. 402.

11. MacMillan, 2001.

12. Bowman, 1928.

13. Black Book. Pg. 27–28.

14. Ibid. Pg. 24.

15. See FRUS Vol. VI. Pg. 678, 687–688.

16. Black Book. Pg. 33–34.

17. Treaty of St. Germain, Article 53.

18. Paul Mowrer. 1921. *Balkanized Europe: A Study in Political Analysis and Reconstruction*. New York: E.P. Dutton & Co.

19. Bowman, 1928. Pg. 333.

20. Black Book. Pg. 30–31.

21. Ibid. Pg. 31.

22. William Westermann. 1921. "The Armenian Problem and the Disruption of Turkey," in *What Really Happened at Paris: The Story of the Peace Conference, 1918–1919 by American Delegates*, ed. Edward House. New York: Charles Scribner's Sons. Pg. 189.

23. Westermann, 1921.

24. Bullitt Lowry. 1996. *Armistice 1918*. Kent, OH: Kent State Press.

25. Westermann, 1921. Pg. 178.

26. Address of President Wilson to Congress, January 8, 1918. In Arthur Link. 1984. *The Papers of Woodrow Wilson, Volume 45*. Princeton, Princeton University Press. Pg. 536.

27. Black Book. Pg. 30.

28. Westermann, 1921. Pg. 178.

29. Leo Dillon. 2005. "The State Department's Office of the Geographer: History and Current Activities." *The Portolan* (64).

30. Hudson, 1921.

31. MacMillan, 2001.

32. Black Book. Pg. 66.

33. Ibid. Pg. 69–70.

34. Bowman, 1921. Pg. 173.

35. Westermann, 1921.Pg. 194.

36. Bowman, 1928. Pg. 403–404.

37. Lawrence Gelfand. 1963. *The Inquiry: American Preparations for Peace 1917–1919*. New Haven: Yale University Press. Pg. 248.

38. Black Book. Pg. 74–75.

39. Hugh Seton-Watson. 1977. *Nations and States: An Enquiry into the Origins of Nations and the Politics of Nationalism*. Boulder, CO: Westview Press. Pg. 262.

40. David Newman. 2005. "Conflict at the Interface: The Impact of Boundaries and Borders on Contemporary Ethnonational Conflict," in Colin Flint, *The Geography of War and Peace: From Death Camps to Diplomats*. Oxford: Oxford University Press. Pg. 332.

41. Black Book. Pg. 77.

42. Ibid. Pg. 78–80.

43. Westermann, 1921.

44. Arthur Walworth. 1986. *Wilson and His Peacemakers: American Diplomacy at the Paris Peace Conference, 1919*. New York: W.W. Norton and Company.

45. Westermann, 1921.

46. For example, see Andelman, 2008. Pg. 62.

47. Black Book. Pg. 81–83.

CHAPTER 6

Legacies of the American Inquiry & the Paris Peace Conference

The repercussions of the Paris Peace Conference continue to be felt today. The conference faced a daunting challenge, trying to bring peace after a war that had spread far beyond the shores of Europe. The problems they had to solve were more complex than those of any preceding time, dealing with more than just unequal territorial divisions, but also with universal unrest from the rise of nationalism, communism and new ideologies such as self-determination.[1] The continued importance placed on the principles of Woodrow Wilson, especially with regard to national self-determination, remain with us today.

For the United States, the negotiating process proved exceptionally difficult. Unlike later periods of the 20th century, in 1919 the United States was not significantly stronger than the European powers. As such, President Wilson possessed less clout to impose his new world vision upon the other Allied powers. As just one of four Great Powers at the peace table, it proved impossible for Wilson to force the Fourteen Points onto Britain, France and Italy as the sole basis of the final peace. Also, the Fourteen Points were relatively murky, so acceptance of them by the Allied states meant very little. Although many aspects of the final treaties, most notably the creation of the League of Nations and some of the territorial settlements, did reflect the Fourteen Points, other parts of the settlement deviated drastically from the American plan. After departing Paris, Colonel Edward House, one of Wilson's closest confidantes in negotiations, pointed to three major accomplishments he felt had emerged from the conference: 1) the formation of the League of Nations, 2) a sincere effort to give self-determination to various peoples, and 3) the application of the trusteeship principle to the new mandate territories.[2] These accomplishments have been largely overshadowed in the intervening years by the failures that also emerged in the final peace settlements. Many of these were unavoidable problems, rather than problems truly created through malice by the negotiating parties. As Charles Seymour, a member of the American delegation noted:

> The Peace Conference, representing the democracies, reflected the mind of the age; it could not rise measurably above its source. That mind was dominated by a reactionary nostalgia and a traditional nationalism.[3]

Although Great Power politicking prevailed in many cases, it must be remembered that the democratically elected leaders of Britain, France and Italy were accountable to their populations, just as Wilson was to the American public. These states had paid a price in blood and money far higher than that paid by the United States during World War I. Thus, the settlements they pushed for reflected the views of their people based on a very different experience, facing war in the case of France and Italy that was mostly fought on their own soil, rather than overseas.

The peace settlements reshaped the map of the world, most dramatically altering Europe. Europe grew from 26 to 38 independent states, and worldwide, the total length of international borders grew by 12,500 miles.[4] As can be seen by analysis of the major border changes envisioned and drawn at the Paris Peace Conference, many means were attempted to draw new borders based upon scientific methods including census data, new surveying techniques and local plebiscites. However, the peacemakers were handicapped in that much of the data, especially census information, they relied upon to make border determinations was long outdated by the time of the conference.[5]

The sheer amount of border drawing also forced the peacemakers to rush through many decisions to complete the treaties in a rapid amount of time, and some borders did not rely upon the scientific method outlined above. Early discussions in different committees and among the Big Four at the conference were supposed to be preliminary, when in actuality these suggestions in many cases became the definitive terms of peace.[6] Outside events, such as the Russian Revolution, also greatly complicated the process of settling many borders. The ethnic mixture of peoples, especially in Eastern Europe, made this process even more difficult, and the territorial settlements remain most important in how they have shaped ongoing conflict stemming from the war.[7]

SIZING UP THE TERRITORIAL SETTLEMENTS

Some of the border changes made in Paris were effected due to the war, such as the transfer of Alsace-Lorraine from France to Germany. Many others, especially those created by the breakup of the Austro-Hungarian Empire, would probably have occurred without the border drawing of the Paris Peace Conference, as the rise of nationalism in the Balkans and Eastern Europe threatened to tear the Hapsburg Empire apart. The Empire would not have lasted long, even had World War I had not broken out despite attempts by the Hapsburgs to accommodate the myriad nationalities of their state and create a more equal status for different constituent groups in the Empire.[8] The breakup of Austria granted eight national groups freedom from the bonds of the dual monarchy, and six new states were created. Similarly, the breakup of the Ottoman Empire led to a dramatic reorganization of territory, but in the case of the new Middle Eastern mandates to Britain and France, the end result was simply a change to new imperial hands, rather than self-determination for those Ottoman subject peoples.

Some of the more troublesome border problems emerging from the peace conference manifested themselves immediately, while it took many decades for other problems to present. Herbert Hoover, a delegate at the peace conference prior to serving as President of the United States, recalled a conversation from May 7, 1919, the day the Treaty of Versailles was presented, with Jan Smuts and John Maynard Keynes, "We agreed that the consequences of many parts of the proposed Treaty would ultimately bring destruction."[9] Keynes went so far as to declare the final treaty a "total failure" only one year after its completion.[10] In many ways they sensed the peace settlement from the "War to End All Wars" would fail to accomplish that lofty goal, a goal for world peace that remains as elusive today as it was in 1919. The final Treaty of Versailles failed to fulfill many of Woodrow Wilson's standards. This problem led to widespread disappointment in America, as it was felt that Wilson failed to eliminate the conditions from Europe that led to the war's initial outbreak.[11] Wilson had been forced into a corner on many issues, especially war reparations. Hans Morgenthau notes, "In the end Wilson had to consent to a series of uneasy compromises which were a betrayal of his moral principles… and which satisfied nobody's national aspirations."[12] Many in Wilson's own delegation were unhappy with the settlements as written. Secretary of State Lansing remarked, "The terms of peace appear immeasurably harsh and humiliating, while many of them are incapable of performance."[13] This was especially evident the further east one looked at the peace settlements. Although the boundaries were supposed to be redrawn through treaties and plebiscites, the easternmost boundaries in Europe were drawn through force, such as the border between Poland and the Soviet Union which emerged after further fighting between these countries. These more eastern boundaries have also proven in many cases to be less permanent than those crafted to the west, those clearly demarcated by the peace treaties.

The failures were partly due to conflicts among the Big Four. Wilson by no means deserves all, or even most of the blame. Although Wilson came to the table with a robust plan for redrawing borders in the Middle East, most of the Middle Eastern settlements were crafted primarily by the British and French delegations without any American involvement. In cases such as this, the Americans had brought boxes of maps and plans, but the perceived lofty impartiality of the American delegation offended the other allies and led to American isolation in the negotiations.[14] The Italians almost shut down the entire conference over their claims in the eastern Adriatic Sea regions, and the settlements finally reached in that region were not even included in the Paris treaties, but had to be set in future agreements between Italy and Yugoslavia, agreements that would be overturned only 25 years later. If one delegation proved the most intransigent, though, it was the French.[15] They rebuffed a host of issues, including reparations and expanding colonial control in the Middle East. In the end, they criticized the treaties in the opposite manner of the other delegations, viewing the treaties as too lenient toward Germany, rather than perceiving the Treaty of Versailles as too harsh.[16] This opinion was validated in the minds of some following the outbreak of World War II, as many scholars believed that Germany was not weakened sufficiently by the Treaty of Versailles.

The problems associated with the peace treaties simmered throughout the interwar period. The relative calm of the twenties gave way to the

Great Depression and the rise of fascism in Europe. Boundary disputes continued during this period, many based on perceived wrongs from the peace treaties, particularly Versailles. The dissolution of the German and Austro-Hungarian Empires had created a situation of almost continuous boundary problems from the Baltic to the Mediterranean Seas. However, many geographers felt that border shifts would, on the whole, do little to improve the political situation on the continent. This change marked a major shift by abandoning border demarcation as the primary peacemaking tool. Exceptions to this included possibly altering the Italian-Austrian border in South Tyrol and adjusting portions of the Hungarian border. Some border adjustments did occur in the interwar period; however, these were imposed on the Allied powers. The capitulation of the French and British to Hitler in 1938 allowing the German annexation of the Sudetenland represents such an example.

Criticism of the final territorial settlements has come from a broad variety of sources in the intervening decades. More than any other factor, it is the failure to create states without large minority populations that has led to this criticism. Potentially, as many as 25 to 30 million people were left as "national minorities" in Eastern Europe alone at the end of World War I, which numbers over a quarter of the total population of the region at the time.[17] The new borders clearly left many people outside their "nation-state," thus leaving the new partition as only a prelude to the next round of conflict. It is not surprising, therefore, that many of the conflicts that erupted later in the 20th century grew out of the territorial settlements. The criticisms of these territorial shifts often point to "mostly artificial" boundaries coming into existence as part of the peace settlement.[18] Such criticism ignores the fact that all borders are artificial and the ability to draw a perfect border is practically nil, with the myriad factors that go into demarcating any international boundary. Unfortunately, the rhetoric, and indeed even the scientific consensus of the time, believed in the possibility to draw such "perfect" borders.

Minorities in the newly formed states quickly created nationalisms of their own. A dynamic emerged from the Paris treaties with three parts: national minorities, newly nationalizing states in which they lived, and the external national homelands to which they belonged by ethno-cultural ties, although not necessarily by citizenship.[19] These interrelated forces made the minority problem one that exacerbated irredentism (the desire of a group to have their territory transferred to a neighboring state), thus leading to territorial revisionism on a broad scale. Border problems created in these settlements festered, in many cases, throughout the entire Cold War period. The recent breakups of Czechoslovakia and Yugoslavia attest to World War I–created borders that remained problematic for many decades.

Many of the ethnic minority problems created at the Paris Peace Conference and in the intervening period persist to this day. There remain enormous ethnic minority populations outside their respective nation-states throughout Europe, particularly in the east. Current major groups include: three million Hungarians (in Romania, Slovakia, Serbia and Ukraine), two million Albanians (in Serbia, Montenegro and Macedonia), two million Serbs (in Bosnia and Croatia), one million Turks (in Bulgaria), Armenians in Azerbaijan, Poles in Lithuania and countless other examples.[20] In the Middle East, similar problems exist, especially the cases of the Kurds and Palestinians, but including many other ethnic groups as well.

The World War I treaties deserve credit for establishing the political geography of Europe for the remainder of the 20th century. Winston Churchill, British Secretary of State for War and Air during the peace conference, viewed the three most important legacies of the treaties being the dissolution of the Austro-Hungarian Empire, the rebirth of Poland and the preservation of a united Germany, all three being territorial parts of the settlements.[21] Churchill noted, "The map of Europe has for the first time been drawn in general harmony with the wishes of its people."[22] He was aware of problems inherent in these settlements, especially the choice of language as the proof of someone's nationality, since it was not always the best indicator, but noted the peace brought forth was in many places as exacting as could be accomplished under the circumstances of the time.

Merely a little over a year after the conference, American plenipotentiary Colonel Edward House remarked on the perceived accomplishments of his delegation at Paris:

> But in spite of unfortunate mistakes in details, it remains true that for the first time in history Europe enjoys a natural political map or, at least, a fair approximation to it, a map drawn in accordance with the unforced aspirations and the spontaneous affiliations of the peoples themselves.[23]

He was clearly aware of the problems that would emerge later in the settlements, but remained strongly supportive of the work done by the Inquiry and at the conference itself. As the previous border studies suggest, large parts of the re-drawing of Europe's map survived long past the conference, including a huge number of borders that remain stable to this day. In the areas where the Inquiry and other experts, rather than the Big Four, played a larger role, the stability of the borders and their relative success in following Wilsonian principles has been much higher. Charles Seymour, a member of the Inquiry, noted:

> [W]here the geographers were given a relatively free hand, as in the European territorial commissions, the Wilsonian program accomplished a higher degree of success than has generally been realized. The frontiers of the new map of Europe conformed more closely with ethnographic divisions than any in previous history.[24]

Borders such as those created for Finland and the Baltic states or the adjustments made to the Danish-German border stand as perfect examples of this assertion. Not only do these show areas where the territorial commissions had an especially strong influence on the re-drawing of the map, but also serve as powerful examples of places where the plans made by the Inquiry were adopted and have proven to stand the test of time, with the Baltic states reemerging after having been absorbed by the Soviet Union during World War II.

Prior to the Paris Peace Conference, Inquiry geographer Douglas Johnson wrote that peace treaties often end up as the *cassus belli* of a new war, because often the peace imposes upon the belligerent illogical and geographically impossible boundaries.[25] He had hoped the World War I settlements would avoid this pitfall. However, the outbreak of World War II is the most oft-cited attribution of the failure of these treaties. The World War I settlements are commonly viewed as the seed for the Second World War. More specifically and correctly, World War II erupted due to the German advancement of historical claims related to the World War I settlements.[26] Adolf Hitler used the Treaty of Versailles as a boogeyman in his political rhetoric, arguing it was a primary cause of Germany's problems. He justified the invasion of Poland in 1939 as righting one of those wrongs by reclaiming the Polish Corridor to the

Baltic Sea to re-link East Prussia with the rest of Germany. Although Hitler's actions did indict the Paris peace treaties, this particular result was not a foregone conclusion at the time of their adoption. Rather, in hindsight, it has been pointed to as such.

Much can be said about perceived failures coming out of the treaties. Indeed, many new borders created large minority populations, but in comparison with the pre–World War I map, where large multiethnic empires were the rule in much of Europe, the new borders did a much better job of approximating the ethno-linguistic divisions of peoples than those prior to the war. Significant attention has been devoted to examining the treaties' failures. But little has been written about paths that might have been chosen instead. Many plans brought to the table by the United States never were negotiated, at least not with American involvement. One must wonder at the difference in regional stability that would have resulted, had more of the Black Book been implemented. Although far from perfect, the American plan hewed more closely to the ethno-linguistic boundaries than did the final settlements.

Despite assertions of failure, the European map that emerged from the Paris Peace Conference was far better than that with which it preceded. American Chief Geographer Isaiah Bowman noted after the end of the next great conflict, World War II, that "Probably no major peace settlement came nearer the mark of principle than the European territorial settlements of 1919."[27] In his reflections on the geographical work done in Paris, Bowman also noted, "Whatever faults they may have the territorial settlements are acknowledged by even the most destructive critics to be the best part of the treaty making."[28] This was seconded by Paul Birdsall in his analysis of the territorial settlements done in 1960:

> Finally, the territorial settlement contained in the various treaties negotiated at Paris is still, with all its faults, the closest approximation of an ethnographic map of Europe that has ever been achieved.[29]

The principle of self-determination stood front and center in the American plan. Applying such a concept in practice proved exceptionally difficult and has continued to raise questions in the intervening decades, but the many lasting accomplishments coming from these proposals cannot be denied.

WAS SELF-DETERMINATION POSSIBLE?

The application of self-determination in the drawing of the postwar borders remains controversial. New borders, in general, are met with resistance. This study suggests that the borders that closely hued with Wilsonian principles were less contested, while those that ignored the principles, usually by including large numbers of minorities within, became the most controversial. The principle of self-determination was only taken into account on certain borders, and almost always favored the pro-Entente states over those of the Central Powers. The new boundaries left many people outside the borders of their nation-states. In Europe alone, up to 30 million people became ethnic minorities in their respective states following the peace conference. In some cases this was unavoidable without drawing complex boundaries or forcibly relocating large numbers of people. Certain states lost large numbers of their national groups as well. This was especially true for Germany and Austria, which each found hundreds of thousands of their ethnic kinsmen outside their borders following the settlements. Their delegates to the conference were stunned with the final settlements. Upon presentation of the preliminary treaty, one German delegate in Paris remarked, "This shameful treaty has broken me, for I believed in Wilson until today."[30] Other nationalities received no nation-state at all; certain groups whose political ambitions remained unfulfilled included Slovaks, Croatians and Ukrainians. One of the biggest blunders proved to be the naïve creation of Yugoslavia. This new state was no less a mosaic of peoples than the Hapsburg and Ottoman Empires that it was carved from. Prominent American diplomat Richard Holbrooke viewed this poor decision as a well-meaning mistake of President Wilson's, as he had not intended to create an "artificial" country.[31] In the 1990s, Holbrooke would attempt a fix using Wilson's principles within a relatively small area, Bosnia, where a new line would emerge within the former Yugoslavia, but even this division from the Dayton Accords has proven problematic in practice.

Today's scholarship on minority issues in Europe and the Middle East includes extensive coverage of the state of national groups that remain stranded outside their nation-states. In their seminal work on minority group aspirations, geographers Marvin Mikesell and Alexander Murphy point to the South Tyrol as a major case study, one that owes its problems to the border settlement reached in the 1919 Paris peace accords.[32] This is also evident in Transylvania, where today there remains a strong irredentist movement among Hungarians wishing to see the northern parts of Transylvania returned to Hungary.[33] For certain scholars, this has led to the conclusion that the treaties failed to take into account the principle of self-determination. Sociologist Rogers Brubaker notes:

> The post–World War I settlements, though ostensibly based on the principle of national self-determination, in fact assigned tens of millions of people to nation-states other than "their own" at the same time that they focused unprecedented attention on the national or putatively national quality of both persons and territory.[34]

It is the impossibility, in areas of mixed population, of being able to draw a border that truly follows national lines that has created this problem. Self-determination was seen as progressive, but it did lead to instability and cartographic uncertainty in its application at Paris.[35]

Some critics of Wilson and the treaties believe the idea of self-determination was not even understood by those who were trying to apply it. A fierce critic of Wilson, David Andelman, editor of *World Policy Journal*, states:

> As it turned out, from the moment he proclaimed what immediately became catnip to oppressed people, until he returned home from Paris and tried to sell his fellow citizens on the treaty that had been drafted with barely a gesture to these principles, neither Wilson himself, nor indeed any of those who acted in his name, had any real idea what he meant by self-determination.[36]

As evidenced in both the plans of the Inquiry and in many of the territorial settlements implemented, there was a clear conception of what was meant by self-determination and a concerted effort by the Americans to apply these principles, despite bombastic claims like those made by Andelman and others. It was the difficulties inherent in the application of the principles, not a lack of understanding or a sincere attempt at their application that proved problematic, thus making such critiques unfair and academically dishonest. At first, Wilson did not necessarily conceive of self-determination as logically leading to outright independence (for example, see Point X of the Fourteen Points regarding Austria-Hungary). However, the realities of the time, plus the strategies of the British and French, and the interpretation of his words by minority groups led to his concept morphing into that of national independence.[37] Granting such independence was clearly more complex than Wilson's critics admit to.

One issue that made the application of self-determination so fraught was the problem of scale. Jeremy Crampton points specifically to the question that plagued American planners trying to implement Wilson's vision, "down to what scale could the rights of national self-determination be honored, or up to what scale could they workably be combined?"[38] Tiny pockets of population (such as Germans in eastern regions of the Austro-Hungarian Empire) or even larger populations separated from the main population of their kinsmen (such as Hungarians in Transylvania) proved especially difficult. The lack of contiguous populations made the complete adoption of self-determination impossible, thus leading the Inquiry to select appropriate scales of population to contain within the proposed new borders. The rhetoric could not possibly match the reality in such cases, which has been a source of ongoing criticism, whether fair or not. There was no way to consistently apply the concept of self-determination due to these problems.

Even at that time, experts were not naïve about the difficulties inherent in the application of Wilsonian principles. Writing soon after the conference, American expert Manley Hudson noted:

> Obviously self-determination as a practical measure has very definite limits. In any territory where races are mixed, where numerous languages are spoken, and where different religions are practiced, the fixing of a national boundary is beset with many difficulties.[39]

These problems were not unique to Europe and the Middle East during this period, but have continued to make the application of the principle of self-determination difficult in the intervening years in many other parts of the world. Two principles have overridden self-determination in a wide variety of cases—sovereignty and territorial integrity; this is best seen through the subsequent process of decolonization when whole colonies gained independence as a single political entity, but not minorities within these territories.[40]

Despite the problems inherent in the application, the language of self-determination persists. Claims for independence today from groups as varied as the Tibetans, Palestinians, Chechens, and many others continue to use the language of Wilsonianism in support of their claims. For these groups, territorial solutions are pointed to as the best method to fix their current predicaments. However, as World War I historian Bullit Lowry notes:

> All methods have faults, and perhaps the faults of self-determination were less than the faults of Absolutist diplomacy. But self-determination was no panacea for the territorial ills of the world.[41]

Even in many cases where the Americans brought a proposal to the table based on the principle and it was adopted, problems persisted. Despite these failings, many of which were impossible to avoid due to the complexity of the demography of a region, much survived. In many places the application of self-determination led to a new territorial order, one that was more representative of the populations on the ground than what had existed before. Tomas Masaryk, first President of Czechoslovakia summed up the meaning that Wilsonian principles held for his people following the end of the Paris Peace Conference:

> The Allies proclaimed the principle of equal rights for small nations, and President Wilson defended these rights with his watchword "self-determination." The Peace Treaties codified the fundamental features of this idea.[42]

Not only in the Austro-Hungarian context, but as can be seen in a wide variety of the border changes made and in most of those proposed by the American Inquiry, self-determination was central to the legacy of the United States' involvement and the final treaties drawn in 1919.

THE LEGACY OF THE AMERICAN INQUIRY & ISAIAH BOWMAN

The Inquiry would go on to have major influence beyond that which it exercised in preparation for and during the peace conference. It marked the first such gathering of a large committee of academics working to advise the U.S. government on important international issues. The Inquiry drew from a large number of academic institutions and convened about 150 academics of all stripe and political affiliation (Bowman himself had been a Republican supporter most of his life prior to the Paris Peace Conference, when his allegiance switched to Wilson's Democrats).[43] The Inquiry thus served as a sort of impromptu government sponsored think tank, long before such institutions as the U.S. Institute of Peace were created to play such a role in the American foreign policy establishment.

Although the Inquiry technically only existed until the start of the Paris Peace Conference, it continued to function at the conference as the Bureau of Inquiry Territorial and Trade Adjustments. Following the conference, the U.S. Department of State relied on the advice of geographers, which necessitated a continuation for the Inquiry in a new form. In 1921, Army Major Lawrence Martin (who worked extensively with the Inquiry in Paris) was appointed as the first geographer at the State Department, with the maintenance of the Inquiry's map collection from the Paris Peace Conference among his roles, along with work on determining final borders set out in the Treaty of Sevres—the Turkish settlement.[44] By 1924, the permanence of a geographic advisor to the Secretary of State was codified when Dr. Samuel Boggs was appointed "Geographer" in the Department. This legacy lives on today, as the Office of the Geographer continues to serve as a key advisory office to the Secretary of State.

Wilson's chief territorial advisor and head of the mapping division of the Inquiry, Isaiah Bowman, also contributed immensely to American foreign policy through his involvement in the Inquiry and the Paris Peace Conference.[45] Neil Smith notes:

No one more than Isaiah Bowman applied the ideas of twentieth-century U.S. geography to public ends. Across an extraordinary range of foundational events, he was "present at the creation" of the American Century.[46]

Although Smith is critical of some of the roles played by Bowman in his work with the government, I would argue that this role remains essential for geographers to play in the conduct of foreign policy. It is unfortunate that another Bowman has yet to emerge and play such a crucial role in the shaping of U.S. foreign policy, especially considering the number of territorial and spatial problems that plagued the world after Bowman left the scene, and the countless such problems that face the world today.

Following the conference, Bowman became a founder of the Council on Foreign Relations, publisher of the highly respected *Foreign Affairs* magazine, as well as serving as President of Johns Hopkins University and as an advisor to President Franklin Roosevelt and the Department of State during the Second World War. His work for Roosevelt helped ensure that the same mistakes made at the end of World War I were not repeated at the end of World War II.[47] Bowman had mixed personal feelings regarding the final settlements reached in Paris. He noted, "In this modern closely organized, strongly commercialized world, it is virtually impossible to make a clear-cut distinction between what is right from the standpoint of ethnography, nationalistic sentiment, and abstract justice, and what is fair from the standpoint of economic advantage."[48]

THE LEGACY OF PRESIDENT WOODROW WILSON

Any discussion of the Paris Peace Conference cannot escape consideration of the legacy of perhaps its most famous figure, that of President Woodrow Wilson. The principles outlined by Wilson before the conference changed the dynamics of international relations and our very understanding of the construction of the inter-state system in a dramatic fashion. Prior to World War I, the general rule in a peace settlement was "to the victor go the spoils." Large multiethnic empires dominated most of the globe in this period, as only the mainland Americas were mostly decolonized. However, the language of Wilson has been applied in justifying claims for independence or resistance ever since. Europe saw its most dramatic border re-drawing in the wake of World War I, but areas such as Africa, the Middle East and South Asia witnessed similar shocking changes in the period following World War II, often justified on similar grounds to the breakup of Eastern European empires in 1919. This new conception of territory, that each nation deserves a state, holds resonance today in conflicts across many parts of the globe, most recently with the creation of South Sudan in 2011 and in the ongoing Israeli-Palestinian conflict.

Many generalizations have been made about Wilson's failings at the conference, as the final settlements clearly did not match the expectations he created based upon the program for peace he presented. Such pronouncements, such as the recent work by David Andelman, point to these perceived failings in an unfair manner:

In the end, Versailles proved a colossal failure for Woodrow Wilson, for the United States, and for the future of a world that had hoped it might be governed by principles of freedom and self-determination—even today.[49]

However, these generalizations are based on the final outcome from the Paris Peace Conference rather than on the proposals that Wilson and his delegation brought to the table. In Wilson's own writings, he shows great concern and displeasure over the final settlements reached.[50] Even so, it is also clear that major portions of the settlement were also successful, as evidenced by the number of borders and new states that continue to occupy the world map today.

Those who criticize the President's plans, rather than just the final settlements, show a lack of awareness of what he brought to the table. Writing just after the war, John Maynard Keynes characterized Wilson's plans thus:

> But in fact the President had thought out nothing; when it came to practice his ideas were nebulous and incomplete. He had no plan, no scheme, no constructive ideas whatever for clothing with the flesh of life the commandments which he had thundered from the White House.[51]

As a member of the British delegation, and not party to discussions within the Big Four itself, Keynes had no idea how comprehensive the American plan for peace was. Although there were holes in what Wilson brought to the table, these were relatively small. As noted in the preceding analysis of the American plan, Wilson brought forth a fairly comprehensive plan for peace. Sadly, the early pronouncements of many people who were ignorant of his plans and what actually took place in negotiations have lived on to be repeated in the history books for the following century. These analyses do not match the facts when considering the robust peace plan that Wilson proposed and tried to bring forth in negotiations.

President Wilson did make domestic political blunders while in Paris, which haunted him after the conference's end and complicated his legacy. With his mistrust of Republicans, the President included no major Republican figures in the American delegation. The Republican Party controlled the Senate that would in the end have to ratify the treaties of peace. The President tried to mobilize public opinion in the United States in favor of the treaties after returning from Paris. During his travels around the country promoting ratification of the Treaty of Versailles, he suffered a severe stroke that incapacitated him for much of the remainder of his presidency. The U.S. Senate finally failed to ratify the Treaty of Versailles on March 19, 1920, falling just shy of the two-thirds majority required. The American system of divided government sowed the seeds for this failure to adopt the peace plan.[52] In the coming years, the United States made separate agreements with the Central Powers and never ended up being party to the treaties that bore the mark of President Wilson. He tried desperately to make the 20th century the "American Century," a legacy that would eventually follow, but not without American leadership in international institutions.[53] The failure to ratify the treaties kept the United States out of the League of Nations and marked a shift back to American isolationism that lasted until the Japanese attack on Pearl Harbor in 1941.

Wilsonian principles did not die in 1919. As the 20th century progressed, the mark of Woodrow Wilson on the international system remained strong. American diplomats continued to believe in the moral geography of Wilson that held sway in future territorial decisions made there. Wilson can be seen as the founding father of the search for a new world order, one that has framed subsequent American foreign policy around the goals of a more liberal, internationalist, anti-revolutionary, capitalist, pacific and exceptionalist planet.[54] The principle of self-determination and the rights of minorities play a major role in international relations today. Minority rights now extend to groups that in Wilson's day were not even on the map. Some form of autonomy has been granted to a great number of groups that do not have their own states. Although for a period of time after the Paris Peace Conference it was considered a poor idea to try again to delimit territories to protect nationalities, now internal borders serve as a key protection for many groups. Scholar Bernard Nietschmann noted this shift in practice:

> More indigenous territory has been claimed by maps than by guns. This assertion has a corollary: more indigenous territory can be reclaimed and defended by maps than by guns.[55]

Although there remains a hesitancy to re-draw thousands of miles of international boundaries wholesale, these new methods of granting internal boundaries to disaffected groups can be seen as a maturation of ideas espoused by Woodrow Wilson.

More than any other President, it is the ideas of Woodrow Wilson that have triumphed in how the United States has behaved as a great power.[56] Stanford historian David Kennedy points to Wilson's call for the League of Nations (now embodied in the United Nations) as central to understanding how Wilson believed the world should work and in shaping the world order that now dominates the international system:

> More clearly than his critics, Wilson recognized that the world now bristled with dangers that no single state could contain, even as it shimmered with prospects that could be seized only by states acting together—that it presented threats incubated by emerging technologies, and opportunities generated by the gathering momentum of the Industrial Revolution. Making such a world safe for democracy required more than the comforting counsels of isolation, and more than taking the inherited international order as a given and conducting the business of great-power diplomacy as usual. It required, rather, active engagement with other states to muzzle the dogs of war, suppress weapons of mass destruction, and improve both standards of living and international comity through economic liberalization. Most urgently, it required new institutions that would import into the international arena at least a modicum of the trust, habits of reciprocity, and rule of law that obtained in well-ordered national policies. These were ambitious goals, but they were also realizable, as time would tell.[57]

Whether it was a matter of domestic politics or just that Wilson was ahead of his time is debatable. However, his impacts on what are now international legal norms such as self-determination and multilateralism continue to shape global politics today.

Many Presidents since Wilson owe much to him especially with the idea that America should advance a moral role in international politics; Presidents who have shown such tendencies in their conduct of foreign policy since include Franklin Roosevelt, Jimmy Carter, Ronald Reagan and Bill Clinton.[58] Many scholars misrepresent Wilson as a "dewy-eyed idealist"; however, many of America's most successful and realistic policies have emerged from his ideas.[59]

A LEGACY WITH US TODAY

Not only the legacy of men such as Wilson and Bowman, but also the Paris treaties' legacies themselves reside with us today, for good or ill.

From the moment of their adoption, the final treaties presented in Paris have had a mixed legacy, although the continued importance placed on Wilsonian ideals proves that their impact remains very strong. Despite the specific problems within the treaties, the overall settlement for Europe made many positive changes, especially through the creation of boundaries that more closely coincided with ethnic groupings than any previous peace settlement. The final treaties also honored more of the Fourteen Points than they violated.[60] Despite major altercations over the Adriatic and other areas, many of Wilson's points were fully carried out within the treaties of peace. The League of Nations was created in the Treaty of Versailles, while territorial adjustments such as the creation of Poland and the transfer of Alsace-Lorraine were fully carried out within that same treaty. In 1910, 40 percent of Europe's population was a minority group within its state, and population shifts and border changes starting with those effected at Paris have today left the continent with 15 states with minority populations smaller than 5 percent of the total population.[61] This greatly reduced the risk of ethnically charged civil war in many parts of Europe.

Throughout the 1920s, American and British public opinion swung around to the attitude that the settlements reached at Paris had been unfair to the belligerents. More and more people realized that both sides had suffered immeasurably from the horrors of trench warfare. The publication of the Nobel prize–winning *All Quiet on the Western Front*, by German Erich Maria Remarque, reinforced the suffering of both sides. Remarque commented that although many men escaped the shells, they were "destroyed by the war."[62] The release of archival materials also showed that Germany had not been solely responsible for the war, and that indeed, the Entente states played a major role in the war's outbreak.[63] The lessons from this conflict and the ensuing peace conference were sadly not learned by those in positions of power after World War I.

The end of the Second World War marked a shift in how peace was established. The American's did not bring a set of principles resembling the Fourteen Points to the table, partly due to continued American bitterness over the final outcome of the World War I settlements. The problem of minorities was not addressed at the end of World War II. Rather than new minorities' treaties or other protections for minorities within states, many states expelled or killed off their minority populations following the war. The expulsion of most Germans from Poland

and Czechoslovakia are good examples of this. The map of the world, including that of Europe, underwent many changes following World War II. These new borders did not take populations into account; instead they were based upon crude geopolitical calculations. The Soviet Union moved its border westward and unilaterally moved Poland's western border into purely German areas.[64] The remains of Germany were divided in two, exactly the opposite of what Winston Churchill had termed one of the territorial successes of the World War I settlements.[65] Israel was created out of portions of the British Mandate of Palestine without a Palestinian state emerging next to it. Unfortunately, the World War II settlements learned lessons from World War I failures that led to a much less idealistic peace settlement. This was evidenced especially through the abandonment of the principle of self-determination in many cases, and instead re-drawing borders according to purely strategic interests.

Wilsonian principles did not die with the Second World War, despite the misjudgments in the World War II settlements. As the 20th century progressed, the mark of Woodrow Wilson on the international system remained strong. The founding of the United Nations, with the United States as its main early defender, marked a shift from the isolationism of the immediate post-Wilson era. The UN, as successor to the League of Nations, has lasted longer and extended its mandate well beyond security. Although the UN does not practice collective security in the way the League was supposed to, it has averted or ameliorated many conflicts around the globe. Wilson's vision of "a general association of nations ... for the purpose of affording mutual guarantees of political independence and territorial integrity to great and small states alike," laid out in the fourteenth point remains alive and strong through the auspices of the United Nations.[66] This organization stands as a testament to the fourteenth point of Woodrow Wilson and one of his most enduring legacies.

The world map has been redrawn many times since Wilson's era, particularly in periods such as the end of World War II, postwar decolonization and the end of the Cold War. However, in general, there remains a reluctance to change international boundaries that was not present at the time of the Paris Peace Conference. The decision of the Organization for African Unity to accept colonial boundaries rather than create new ones across Africa reflected the realization that a massive re-demarcation, like the one that occurred in Eastern

Europe after World War I, was an idea that could spark widespread international conflict in Africa. In Wilson's day it was believed that borders could be drawn "scientifically." This idea has not held up to the test of time. Few borders drawn since World War I successfully demonstrated that political borders can be drawn by neutral scientific methods devoid of internal and international political concerns. The concept that "natural" borders even exist has been discredited since Wilson's time.[67] The disastrous partition of British India in 1947 and the failed UN partition plan for Palestine in 1948 both show how difficult it is to attempt to draw borders based on "scientific" information, such as census data in areas with mixed populations, reaffirming the difficulties seen in Transylvania and Istria, among other places, at the end of World War I.

The Paris treaties' legacies reside with us today, for good or ill. Their positive aspects, such as the promulgation of the idea of self-determination, the creation of multilateral organizations as a key part of the international system, and the negative consequences of ongoing border conflicts remain with us today. The importance of these principles to the international system guides the conduct of diplomacy and peacemaking around the world. The United Nations stands as testament to Wilson's belief in international cooperation to solve conflicts, rather than resorting to force. The UN trust territories also fit within this Wilsonian idea, as these were created at the end of World War II and all have since been given the opportunity for independence, much in the way Wilson had anticipated the League of Nations mandates to work. Border changes, both internal and external, continue to reshape the map of the world. The creation of autonomous regions within states shows a remarkable application of Wilsonian ideals in a way not widely envisioned or understood during his lifetime. Although it remains a diplomatic tool of last resort due to its disruptive nature, the re-drawing of international borders continues to be used to ameliorate conflict. It is difficult and reductive to judge the Paris treaties either as failure or success. Isaiah Bowman, himself heavily involved in the crafting of the settlements, reminds us, "It is easy to speculate on what might have been; it was not so easy to draw boundaries at a time when account had to be taken of wartime promises and of the actual state of the political world."[68]

NOTES

1. Isaiah Bowman. 1928. *The New World: Problems in Political Geography*. New York: World Book.

2. Edward House. 1921. "The Versailles Peace in Retrospect," in *What Really Happened at Paris: The Story of the Peace Conference, 1918–1919 by American Delegates*, ed. Edward House. New York: Charles Scribner's Sons. Pg. 425.

3. Charles Seymour. 1960. "Geography, Justice, and Politics at the Paris Conference of 1919," in *The Versailles Settlement: Was It Foredoomed to Failure?* ed. Ivo Lederer. Boston: D.C. Heath and Co. Pg. 110.

4. David Stevenson, 2004. *Cataclysm: The First World War as Political Tragedy*. New York: Basic Books.

5. Julian Minghi. 1963 (ii). "Boundary Studies in Political Geography." *Annals of the Association of American Geographers* (53:3).

6. Stevenson, 2004.

7. Niall Ferguson. 2006. *The War of the World: Twentieth-Century Conflict and the Descent of the West*. New York: Penguin.

8. Mark Mazower. 1998. *Dark Continent: Europe's Twentieth Century*. London: Penguin Press. Pg. 42–44.

Richard Hartshorne. 1950. "The Functional Approach in Political Geography." *Annals of the Association of American Geographers* (40: 2).

9. Herbert Hoover. 1992. *The Ordeal of Woodrow Wilson*. Baltimore: Woodrow Wilson Center. Pg. 234.

10. John M. Keynes. 1920. *The Economic Consequences of the Peace*. New York: Harcourt, Brace and Howe. Pg. 226.

11. Arthur Walworth. 1986. *Wilson and His Peacemakers: American Diplomacy at the Paris Peace Conference, 1919*. New York: W.W. Norton and Company.

12. Hans Morgenthau. 1965. "The National Interest vs. Moral Abstrations," in Edwin Rozwenc and Thomas Lyons, *Realism and Idealism in Wilson's Peace Program*. Boston: DC Heath and Co. Pg. 81.

13. Margaret MacMillan. 2001. *Paris 1919*. New York: Random House. Pg. 467.

14. George Goldberg. 1969. *The Peace to End Peace: The Paris Peace Conference of 1919*. New York: Harcourt, Brace & World, Inc. Pg. 21.

15. MacMillan, 2001.

16. Ibid.

17. Stuart Woolf. 1996. *Nationalism in Europe, 1815 to the Present: A Reader*. London: Routledge. Pg. 25.

18. Amos Perlmutter. 1997. *Making the World Safe for Democracy: A Century of Wilsonianism and Its Totalitarian Challengers*. Chapel Hill: University of North Carolina Press. Pg. 19.

19. Rogers Brubaker. 1996. *Nationalism Reframed: Nationhood and the National Question in the New Europe*. Cambridge: Cambridge University Press. Pg. 4.

20. Ibid. Pg. 56.

21. Winston Churchill. 1960. "The World Crisis: The Territorial Settlements of 1919–1920," in Ido Lederer, *The Versailles Settlement: Was It Foredoomed to Failure?* Boston: DC Heath & Co.

22. Ibid. Pg. 80.

23. House, 1921. Pg. 430.

24. Seymour, 1960. Pg. 113.

25. Douglas Johnson. 1917. "The Role of Political Boundaries." *Geographical Review* (4:3).

26. Alexander Murphy. 1990. "Historical Justifications for Territorial Claims." *Annals of the Association of American Geographers* (80:4).

27. Isaiah Bowman. 1946. "The Strategy of Territorial Decisions." *Foreign Affairs* (24:2).Pg. 182.

28. Isaiah Bowman. *undated*. "The Geographical Program of the American Peace Delegation, 1919." JHU Bowman Papers MS 58 Box 13.3.Pg. 1.

29. Birdsall 1960. Pg. 26.

30. MacMillan, 2001. Pg. 465.

31. Vjekoslav Perica. 2002. *Balkan Idols*. Oxford: Oxford University Press.

32. Marvin Mikesell and Alexander Murphy. 1991. "A Framework for Comparative Study of Minority-Group Aspirations." *Annals of the Association of American Geographers* (81:4).

33. John Cadzow. 1983. *Transylvania: The Roots of Ethnic Conflict*. Kent, OH: Kent State Press.

34. Brubaker, 1996. Pg. 6.

35. Jeremy Black. 1997 (ii). *Maps and Politics*. Chicago: University of Chicago Press. Pg. 143.

36. David Andelman. 2008. *A Shattered Peace: Versailles 1919 and the Price We Pay Today*. Hoboken, NJ: John Wiley & Sons. Pg. 151.

37. George White. 2004. *Nation, State, and Territory: Origins, Evolutions, and Relationships Volume 1*. Lanham, MD: Rowman & Littlefield. Pg. 210.

38. Jeremy Crampton. 2006. "The Cartographic Calculation of Space: Race Mapping and the Balkans at the Paris Peace Conferece of 1919." *Social and Cultural Geography* (7:5). Pg. 747.

39. Manley Hudson. 1921. "The Protection of Minorities and Natives in Transferred Territories," in *What Really Happened at Paris: The Story of the*

Peace Conference, 1918–1919 by American Delegates, ed. Edward House. New York: Charles Scribner's Sons. Pg. 205.

40. David Knight. 1999 (ii). "Rethinking Territory, Sovereignty, and Identities" in *Reordering the World: Geopolitical Perspectives for the 21st Century*, ed. William Wood and George Demko. Boulder, CO: Westview Press.

41. Lowry, 1996. Pg. 30.

42. Thomas Masaryk. 1960. "The Case for the Successor States," in Ido Lederer, *The Versailles Settlement: Was It Foredoomed to Failure?* Boston: DC Heath & Co. Pg. 101.

43. Bowman, *undated*.

44. Leo Dillon. 2005. "The State Department's Office of the Geographer: History and Current Activities." *The Portolan* (64).

45. Two differing accounts of Bowman's legacy each address his impact both in the World War I settlements and beyond. Geoffrey Martin's *The Life & Thought of Isaiah Bowman* views Bowman's impacts as highly influential on the course of American geography and foreign policy, mostly in a positive regard. Neil Smith's *American Empire: Roosevelt's Geographer and the Prelude to Globalization* takes a harder line, looking at many areas in which Smith argues that Bowman was an instrumental figure in shaping many American policies that have reverberated more negatively over the coming years.

46. Neil Smith. 2003. *American Empire: Roosevelt's Geographer and the Prelude to Globalization*. Berkeley: University of California Press. Pg. xx.

47. Brian Blouet. 2001. *Geopolitics and Globalization in the Twentieth Century*. London: Reaktion Books.

48. Quoted in Seymour 1960, Pg. 113.

49. Andelman, 2008. Pg. 284.

50. Walworth, 1986.

51. Keynes, 1920. Pg. 42–43.

52. John Agnew. 2005 (i). *Hegemony: The New Shape of Global Power*. Philadelphia: Temple University Press.

53. P.J. Taylor. 1993 (i). "Geopolitical World Orders," in *Political Geography of the Twentieth Century*, ed. P.J. Taylor. New York: John Wiley & Sons.

54. Perlmutter, 1997. Pg. 5.

55. Bernard Nietschmann. 1995. "Defending Miskito Reefs with Maps and GPS." *Cultural Survival Quarterly* (18:4).

56. David Kennedy. 2010. "What Would Wilson Do?" *The Atlantic* (305:1).

57. Ibid. Pg. 92–93.

58. Perlmutter, 1997.

59. Kennedy, 2010. Pg. 93.

60. Arthur Link. 1965. "Wilson and the Liberal Peace Program," in Edwin Rozwenc and Thomas Lyons, *Realism and Idealism in Wilson's Peace Program*. Boston: DC Heath and Co.

61. John O'Loughlin. 2000. "Ordering the 'Crush Zone': Geopolitical Games in Post–Cold War Eastern Europe," in *Geopolitics at the End of the Twentieth Century* ed. Nurit Kliot and David Newman. New York: John Wiley & Sons.

62. Erich Maria Remarque. 1929. *All Quiet on the Western Front*. New York: Little Brown and Company.

63. MacMillan, 2001.

64. Timothy Snyder. 2003. *The Reconstruction of Nations: Poland, Ukraine, Lithuania, Belarus, 1569–1999*. New Haven: Yale University Press.

65. Churchill, 1960.

66. Address of President Wilson to Congress, January 8, 1918. In Arthur Link. 1984. *The Papers of Woodrow Wilson, Volume 45*. Princeton: Princeton University Press. Pg. 536.

67. Richard Hartshorne. 1950. "The Functional Approach in Political Geography." *Annals of the Association of American Geographers* (40:2).

68. Bowman, 1928. Pg. 32.

CHAPTER 7

Postscript—A World of Nation-States?

The generally accepted historical perspective on American involve-ment in the Paris Peace Conference, and indeed of the ideas of Wood-row Wilson, centers around the perceived failures of the World War I settlements, the beginnings of international organization through the founding of the League of Nations, and the idea of self-determination. However, one feature of the First World War settlements, and a key feature of Wilsonianism, remains sidelined in these discussions—the paradigm shift from a world centered on empires as the main type of political entity to a world of nation-states.

In many respects, World War I can be seen best as a conflict between imperialism and nationalism, in which the nation-state ideal emerged triumphant.[1] However, the war did not start in such a manner. At its outbreak, the Entente Powers included the Russian Empire, a state hold-ing populations from hundreds of nations. Several nations comprised Britain, as well; four within its home territory of the British Isles, and throughout the British Empire hundreds of others. Even France, which within Europe is considered one of the first nation-states, consisted of a vast empire with countless other peoples.[2] Only with the entry of the United States into the war, and the peace program presented by Presi-dent Wilson, did the nation-state ideal really gain any traction as an aim for the peace. Although none of the Fourteen Points calls for the realignment of states from imperial into national, most of the territorial points do suggest adjustments based on lines of nationality, and the fourteenth point, which speaks for the establishment of the League of Nations also specifies that the League will afford "mutual guarantees of political independence and territorial integrity to great and little states alike."[3] Because Wilson envisioned great and little nations alike to have the right to self-determination, it was seen as necessary to protect the rights of these less populous national groups.

Although intimately tied to the idea of self-determination, the evolution of the nation-state ideal ranges further. The American peace plan expressly championed a series of nation-states in Central and Eastern Europe to replace the multiethnic empires that preceded them. Even in the Middle Eastern proposals, the new suggested borders came closer to reflecting this idea than the preceding Ottoman Empire had. Despite the desire to protect smaller nations, it is clear from the American plans that a certain threshold in size and stature was still required to become a state. The American plans predicated both Yugoslavia and Czechoslovakia, despite these entities clearly containing more than one nation within. Yet, the Americans did advocate certain nations with very small populations to gain statehood, such as the Estonians and Latvians. A third category of nations, those considered unready for statehood, were promised mandates under the protection of large powerful states as an interim measure. This idea, that only certain groups of people were ready to govern themselves, reflects the inherent bias and racism of the time. Despite that, it was expected that even these "backward" peoples would eventually be ready for self-governance and would emerge as separate states. After the conference ended, one of the great questions remaining was what the outcome would be of putting the practice of self-determination into force.

This idea of all nation-states, large and small, operating on an equal field is a novel concept, one which in practice has not played out as such. Despite being nominally sovereign, the larger cast of states that emerged from World War I, as well as later waves of creation of new states, has led to a world where all states are anything but equal. As shown by many scholars of nationalism, state sovereignty operates in a variety ways in the modern world, many of which involve only certain aspects of sovereignty applying to all states. International legal sovereignty, the recognition of statehood by other states, is the only form of sovereignty that many of the new "nation-states" created after World War I and in later waves would ever possess fully. The full trappings of statehood, including the ability to control one's territory and exercise sovereignty within it was and is lacking in many of the states that have arisen from the implementation of Wilsonian ideals.

The nation-state concept had been evolving long before the outbreak of the war, but it was only with the peace following that the nation-state system came to fruition.[4] The new system did not differ greatly from the imperial system that preceded it. Rather than the world instantly going from one composed mostly of multinational empires to one of nation-states, the world instead continued to exist as before, only seeing the language of how the state justified itself changing. In the postwar era, states widely adopted terminology that reflected the nation-state ideal, while they continued to violate national sovereignty and behave similarly to states prior to the war.[5]

After the Paris Peace Conference, the United States retreated into isolationism. Just as Wilsonian ideas were highly influential among some American foreign policy thinkers, isolationist strains were equally American in origin, as many Americans in the West and Midwest especially perceived the United States as a refuge from rather than a beacon of hope to the rest of the world.[6] For two decades the isolationists would dominate. Despite Wilsonian ideals receding in American foreign policy right after the war, these ideas emerged into the forefront of American foreign policy after World War II, when the United States came to serve as the great champion of rights and democracy around the world. Many of the peoples and places untouched in the Paris negotiations began to emerge as independent entities during the period of decolonization, and as these new states emerged, they suffused their claims for independence with Wilsonian rhetoric and the language of the nation-state. No longer was it acceptable to present one's state with the sorts of language and titles that had been almost universal prior to World War I. European states, themselves using such language at home, were no longer able to hold back the tide as the world map evolved with the proliferation of the number of states. Prior to World War I, there were barely 50 states around the globe; by 1950 that number had risen to over 75, and today to almost 200. The United States was certainly not alone in championing the cause of these states, but was one power intimately involved, partly due to American support for the rights of peoples to govern themselves.

Despite this, the world map comes nowhere close to resembling a map of nations. The term nation-state implies that the state will represent a single people and serve as their homeland, while excluding large numbers of people that belong to other nations. The aspirations of several thousand nations are not represented by the current makeup of states and only a handful of states can truly be characterized as a nation-state in the world today.[7] The challenge of creating a true nation-state can easily be seen through the problems encountered by the Inquiry as they first tried to forge a new European territorial order based on ethno-linguistic characteristics. Populations are rarely, if ever, homogenous. In the lands of the German, Austro-Hungarian, Russian and Ottoman Empires, those lands that saw the most massive territorial shifts in the post–World War I era populations were incredibly diffuse and mixed. Without creating a series of states that functioned as "islands" of people all mixed together with no territorial integrity, it would be impossible to divide the map in a way that would accurately create nation-states in these regions. As other borders emerged through the process of decolonization and through the breakup of the Soviet Union and Yugoslavia, the same problem occurred again. New states came onto the world scene claiming to represent a nation, but in reality they controlled space occupied by many peoples.

The true shift has not been to a world of nation-states, but rather can be seen as a paradigm shift in how the world has been viewed politically and how the language that states use to present themselves has changed. Wilsonian ideals created a context whereby the very way in which states present themselves and the ways in which we perceive states has been altered dramatically. Most states today, regardless of their makeup or actual political system, present themselves as "republics," usually that refer to a people or peoples within the state in the very name they adopt as their full title. The paradigm shift can further be seen in the titles of the two most important international organizations to have emerged, first with the League of Nations and then after World War II with the United Nations, both of which are organizations of states, certainly not of nations. The UN General Assembly presents itself as a gathering of the nations of the world when it convenes each year, however, there would need to be thousands of seats rather than the 193 there are today. Despite these contradictions, the language of the nation-state is all pervasive. People mistakenly use the word nation as a synonym for state and have come to think of states as somehow representing nations.

The language of the nation-state has become central in the manner in which we discuss the world political system today. This paradigm shift began with the World War I settlements and what Woodrow Wilson brought to the table in Paris. Although far from creating such a world then, or even now, the language of that nation-state remains. At the start of the 21st century, some have suggested that the nation-state system is in decline, but the end of this basic structure of global political organization is nowhere in sight.[8] If one legacy stands above all others from the Paris Peace Conference, it is this basic change in how we perceive and describe the world political system. We certainly do not live in a world of true nation-states today, and likely never will. We do, however, live in a world that presents itself and legitimizes its political organization through this idea, one that first came into the norm with the American plan for peace presented in 1919.

NOTES

1. George White. 2004. *Nation, State, and Territory: Origins, Evolutions, and Relationships Volume 1.* Lanham, MD: Rowman & Littlefield. Pg. 176.

2. For a discussion on the historic emergence of the nation-state and nationalism, see: Eric Hobsbawm. 1990. *Nations and Nationalism since 1780: Programme, Myth, Reality.* Cambridge: Cambridge University Press.

3. Address of President Wilson to Congress, January 8, 1918. In Arthur Link. 1984. *The Papers of Woodrow Wilson, Volume 45.* Princeton: Princeton University Press. Pg. 536.

4. Neil Smith. 2003. *American Empire: Roosevelt's Geographer and the Prelude to Globalization.* Berkeley: University of California Press. Pg. 118.

5. Alexander Murphy. 1999. "International Law and the Sovereign State System," in *Reordering the World: Geopolitical Perspectives for the 21st Century,* ed. William Wood and George Demko. Boulder, CO: Westview Press. Pg. 229.

6. Peter Trubowitz. 1998. *Defining the National Interest: Conflict and Change in American Foreign Policy.* Chicago: University of Chicago Press. Pg. 91–95.

7. William Wood and George Demko. 1999. "Political Geography for the Next Millennium," in *Reordering the World: Geopolitical Perspectives for the 21st Century*, ed. William Wood and George Demko. Boulder, CO: Westview Press. Pg. 8.

8. Nuala Johnson. 2002. "The Renaissance of Nationalism," in *Geographies of Global Change*, ed. R.J. Johnston, Peter Taylor, and Michael Watts. Oxford: Blackwell. Pg. 141.

A Note About the
Primary Source Materials

Although there are countless sources that can be consulted regarding the American preparations for peace and how these were then negotiated, a relatively small number offer the specific information needed to conduct this research. The author consulted two copies of "The Black Book," both the manuscript copy which includes the original inked lines on the draft maps, which resides in the Bowman Papers at Johns Hopkins University and also the copy in the Miller Diary. The copy of the Miller Diary at the Department of State was used, this is the 40th of 40 copies printed and only left the library stacks once, for use in this research. Both the State Department and Hopkins documents offer especially compelling material, in that they remained unavailable until quite recently. The Paris Peace Conference series in the Bowman Papers was not available when most research on Bowman was done, including the work by Geoffrey Martin in the 1970s and 1980s. Only Neil Smith's recent work on Bowman has extensively used these documents prior to this research, yet Smith focuses more on Bowman's later work for FDR than his work with the Inquiry. The State Department holdings remain, to this day, only available to Department employees, giving this author firsthand access to materials that, although also available at the National Archives, are untouched by previous researchers in their original form. Because many others have written on the Paris Peace Conference from countless other primary sources, this research has focused on these rare documents and relied heavily on the excellent previous work of other scholars. Of special importance here is the work of the Department of State's Historians Office. This office compiles

the volumes "Foreign Relations of the United States." Rather than using and potentially damaging original manuscript copies of telegrams,
meeting notes and briefing papers held at the National Archives, using
these reproduced and indexed copies allows the researcher full access
to the documents used at the Paris Peace Conference by the American
delegation without having to spend countless hours in the National Archives digging through thousands of feet of documents preserved from
the conference. To the work of these scholars, I am most indebted in
being able to carry out this research.

Bibliography

Agnew, John. 1993. "The United States and American Hegemony." In *Political Geography of the Twentieth Century*, ed. P.J. Taylor. New York: John Wiley & Sons.

Agnew, John. 1998. *Geopolitics: Re-Visioning World Politics*. New York: Routledge.

Agnew, John. 2005. *Hegemony: The New Shape of Global Power*. Philadelphia: Temple University Press.

Andelman, David. 2008. *A Shattered Peace: Versailles 1919 and the Price We Pay Today*. Hoboken, NJ: John Wiley & Sons.

Anderson, Benedict. 1991. *Imagined Communities*. London: Verso.

Baker, Ray. 1922. *Woodrow Wilson and World Settlement Vol. III*. Garden City NY: Doubleday, Page & Co.

Birdsall, Paul. 1960. "Versailles Twenty Years After—A Defense." In Ido Lederer, *The Versailles Settlement: Was It Foredoomed to Failure?*. Boston: DC Heath & Co.

Black, Jeremy. 1997. *Maps and History: Constructing Images of the Past*. New Haven: Yale University Press.

Black, Jeremy. 1997. *Maps and Politics*. Chicago: University of Chicago Press.

Blouet, Brian. 2001. *Geopolitics and Globalization in the Twentieth Century*. London: Reaktion Books.

Bowman, Isaiah. 1921. "Constantinople and the Balkans." In *What Really Happened at Paris: The Story of the Peace Conference, 1918–1919 by American Delegates*, ed. Edward House. New York: Charles Scribner's Sons.

Bowman, Isaiah. 1928. *The New World: Problems in Political Geography*. New York: World Book.

Bowman, Isaiah. 1946. "The Strategy of Territorial Decisions." *Foreign Affairs* (24:2).

Bowman, Isaiah. *undated*. "The Geographical Program of the American Peace Delegation, 1919." JHU Bowman Papers MS 58 Box 13.3.

Brigham, Albert Perry. 1919. "Principles in the Determination of Boundaries." *Geographical Review* (4:7).

Brubaker, Rogers. 1992. *Citizenship and Nationhood in France and Germany*. Cambridge, MA: Harvard University Press.

Brubaker, Rogers. 1996. *Nationalism Reframed: Nationhood and the National Question in the New Europe*. Cambridge: Cambridge University Press.

Brubaker, Rogers. 1997. "Aftermaths of Empire and the Unmixing of Peoples." In Karen Barkey and Mark von Hagen, *After Empire: Multi-Ethnic Societies and Nation-Building*. Boulder, CO: Westview Press.

Cadzow, John. 1983. *Transylvania: The Roots of Ethnic Conflict*. Kent, OH: Kent State Press.

Callender, Harold. 1927. "Alsace-Lorraine Since the War." *Foreign Affairs* (5:3).

Churchill, Winston. 1960. "The World Crisis: The Territorial Settlements of 1919–1920." In Ido Lederer, *The Versailles Settlement: Was It Foredoomed to Failure?*. Boston: DC Heath & Co.

Crampton, Jeremy. 2003. "Can We Learn from the Paris Peace Conference of 1919?" *Geoworld*. http://www.geoplace.com/gw/2003/0310/0310last.asp (accessed April 8, 2006)

Crampton, Jeremy. 2006. "The Cartographic Calculation of Space: Race Mapping and the Balkans at the Paris Peace Conferece of 1919." *Social and Cultural Geography* (7:5).

Cvijic, Jovan. 1918. "The Geographical Distribution of the Balkan Peoples." *Geographical Review* (5:5).

Dillon, Leo. 2005. "The State Department's Office of the Geographer: History and Current Activities." *The Portolan* (64).

Dominian, Leon. 1915. "Linguistic Areas in Europe: Their Boundaries and Political Significance." *Bulletin of the American Geographical Society* (47:6).

Dominian, Leon. 1917. *Frontiers of Language and Nationality in Europe*. New York: Henry Holt and Company.

Dominian, Leon. 1918. "The Nationality Map of Europe." In *League of Nations*. Boston: World Peace Foundation.

Elcock, Howard. 1972. *Portrait of a Decision: The Council of Four and the Treaty of Versailles*. Birkenhead, UK: Eyre Methuen Ltd.

Ferguson, Niall. 2006. *The War of the World: Twentieth-Century Conflict and the Descent of the West*. New York: Penguin.

Gelfand, Lawrence. 1963. *The Inquiry: American Preparations for Peace 1917–1919*. New Haven: Yale University Press.

George, Robert. 1927. "Eupen and Malmedy." *Foreign Affairs* (5:2).

Goldberg, George. 1969. *The Peace to End Peace: The Paris Peace Conference of 1919*. New York: Harcourt, Brace & World, Inc.

Hartshorne, Richard. 1933. "Geographic and Political Boundaries in Upper Silesia." *Annals of the Association of American Geographers* (23:4).

Hartshorne, Richard. 1937. "The Polish Corridor." *The Journal of Geography* (36:5).

Hartshorne, Richard. 1938. "A Survey of the Boundary Problems of Europe." In Charles Colby, *Geographic Aspects of International Relations*. Chicago: University of Chicago.

Hartshorne, Richard. 1950. "The Functional Approach in Political Geography." *Annals of the Association of American Geographers* (40:2).

Haskins, Charles. 1921. "The New Boundaries of Germany." In *What Really Happened at Paris: The Story of the Peace Conference, 1918–1919 by American Delegates*, ed. Edward House. New York: Charles Scribner's Sons.

Held, Colbert. 1951. "The New Saarland." *Geographical Review* (41:4).

Hill, Norman. 1945. *Claims to Territory in International Law and Relations*. London: Oxford University.

Hoffman, George W. 1954. "Boundary Problems in Europe." *Annals of the Association of American Geographers* (44:1).

Hoover, Herbert. 1992. *The Ordeal of Woodrow Wilson*. Baltimore: Woodrow Wilson Center.

House, Edward. 1921. "The Versailles Peace in Retrospect." In *What Really Happened at Paris: The Story of the Peace Conference, 1918–1919 by American Delegates*, ed. Edward House. New York: Charles Scribner's Sons.

Hudson, Manley. 1921. "The Protection of Minorities and Natives in Transferred Territories." In *What Really Happened at Paris: The Story of the Peace Conference, 1918–1919 by American Delegates*, ed. Edward House. New York: Charles Scribner's Sons.

Johnson, Douglas. 1917. "The Role of Political Boundaries." *Geographical Review* (4:3).

Johnson, Douglas. 1921. "Fiume and the Adriatic Problem." In *What Really Happened at Paris: The Story of the Peace Conference, 1918–1919 by American Delegates*, ed. Edward House. New York: Charles Scribner's Sons.

Johnson, Nuala. 2002. "The Renaissance of Nationalism." In *Geographies of Global Change*, ed. R.J. Johnston, Peter Taylor, and Michael Watts. Oxford: Blackwell.

Kennedy, David. 2010. "What Would Wilson Do?" *The Atlantic* (305:1).

Kennedy, Paul. 1987. *The Rise and Fall of the Great Powers*. New York: Random House.

Kern, Stephen. 1983. *The Culture of Time and Space: 1880–1918*. Cambridge, MA: Harvard University Press.

Keynes, John M. 1920. *The Economic Consequences of the Peace*. New York: Harcourt, Brace and Howe.

Knight, David. 1982. "Identity and Territory: Geographical Perspectives on Nationalism and Regionalism." *Annals of the Association of American Geographers*, (72:4).

Knight, David. 1999. "Rethinking Territory, Sovereignty, and Identities." In *Reordering the World: Geopolitical Perspectives for the 21st Century*, ed. William Wood and George Demko. Boulder, CO: Westview Press.

Laponce, J.A. 2004. "Turning Votes into Territories: Boundary Referendums in Theory and Practice." *Political Geography* (23:2).

Link, Arthur. 1965. "Wilson and the Liberal Peace Program." In Edwin Rozwenc and Thomas Lyons, *Realism and Idealism in Wilson's Peace Program*. Boston: DC Heath and Co.

Liulevicius, Vejas. 2000. *War Land on the Eastern Front: Culture, National Identity, and German Occupation in World War I*. Cambridge: Cambridge University Press.

Lord, Robert. 1921. "Poland." In *What Really Happened at Paris: The Story of the Peace Conference, 1918–1919 by American Delegates*, ed. Edward House. New York: Charles Scribner's Sons.

Lowry, Bullitt. 1996. *Armistice 1918*. Kent, OH: Kent State Press.

MacMillan, Margaret. 2001. *Paris 1919*. New York, Random House.

Martin, Geoffrey. 1968. *Mark Jefferson: Geographer*. Ypsilanti, MI: Eastern Michigan University Press.

Martin, Geoffrey. 1980. *The Life and Thought of Isaiah Bowman*. Hamden: Archon Books.

Masaryk, Thomas. 1960. "The Case for the Successor States." In Ido Lederer, *The Versailles Settlement: Was It Foredoomed to Failure?*. Boston: DC Heath & Co.

Mazower, Mark. 1998. *Dark Continent: Europe's Twentieth Century*. London: Penguin.

Mezes, Sidney. 1921. "Preparations for Peace." In *What Really Happened at Paris: The Story of the Peace Conference, 1918–1919 by American Delegates*, ed. Edward House. New York: Charles Scribner's Sons.

Mikesell, Marvin, and Alexander Murphy. 1991. "A Framework for Comparative Study of Minority-Group Aspirations." *Annals of the Association of American Geographers* (81:4).

Minghi, Julian. 1963. "Boundary Studies in Political Geography." *Annals of the Association of American Geographers* (53:3).

Morgenthau, Hans. 1965. "The National Interest vs. Moral Abstrations." In Edwin Rozwenc and Thomas Lyons, *Realism and Idealism in Wilson's Peace Program*. Boston: DC Heath and Co.

Mowrer, Paul. 1921. *Balkanized Europe: A Study in Political Analysis and Reconstruction*. New York: E.P. Dutton & Co.

Murphy, Alexander. 1990. "Historical Justifications for Territorial Claims." *Annals of the Association of American Geographers* (80:4).

Murphy, Alexander. 1999. "International Law and the Sovereign State System." In *Reordering the World: Geopolitical Perspectives for the 21st Century*, ed. William Wood and George Demko. Boulder, CO: Westview Press.

Newman, David. 2005. "Conflict at the Interface: The Impact of Boundaries and Borders on Contemporary Ethnonational Conflict." In Colin Flint, *The Geography of War and Peace: From Death Camps to Diplomats*. Oxford: Oxford University Press.

Nicolson, Harold. 1933. *Peacemaking 1919*. London: Constable & Co.

Nicolson, Harold. 1964. *Peacemaking, 1919*. London: Simon Publications.

Nietschmann, Bernard. 1995. "Defending Miskito Reefs with Maps and GPS." *Cultural Survival Quarterly* (18:4).

O'Loughlin, John. 2000. "Ordering the 'Crush Zone': Geopolitical Games in Post–Cold War Eastern Europe." In Nurit Kliot and David Newman, *Geopolitics at the End of the Twentieth Century*. London: Frank Cass.

O'Loughlin, John, and Herman van der Wusten. 1993. "Political Geography of War and Peace." In *Political Geography of the Twentieth Century*, ed. P.J. Taylor. New York: John Wiley & Sons.

Patten, Simon. 1915. "Unnatural Boundaries of European States." *Survey* (34).

Perica, Vjekoslav. 2002. *Balkan Idols*. Oxford: Oxford University Press.

Perlmutter, Amos. 1997. *Making the World Safe for Democracy: A Century of Wilsonianism and Its Totalitarian Challengers*. Chapel Hill: University of North Carolina Press.

Reisser, Wesley. 2009. "Self-Determination and the Difficulty of Creating Nation-States-The Transylvania Case." *Geographical Review* (99:2).

Remarque, Erich Maria. 1929. *All Quiet on the Western Front*. New York: Little Brown and Company.

Rozwenc, Edwin, and Thomas Lyons. 1965. *Realism and Idealism in Wilson's Peace Program*. Boston: DC Heath and Co.

Scriven, George. 1919. "The Awakening of Albania." *Geographical Review* (8:2).

Seton-Watson, Hugh. 1977. *Nations and States: An Enquiry into the Origins of Nations and the Politics of Nationalism*. Boulder, CO: Westview Press.

Seymour, Charles. 1921. "The End of an Empire: Remnants of Austria-Hungary." In *What Really Happened at Paris: The Story of the Peace Conference, 1918–1919 by American Delegates*, ed. Edward House. New York: Charles Scribner's Sons.

Seymour, Charles. 1960. "Geography, Justice, and Politics at the Paris Conference of 1919." In *The Versailles Settlement: Was It Foredoomed to Failure?* ed. Ivo Lederer. Boston: D.C. Heath and Co.

Simonds, Frank. 1927. *How Europe Made Peace Without America*. Garden City: Doubleday, Page and Co.

Smith, Neil. 2003. *American Empire: Roosevelt's Geographer and the Prelude to Globalization*. Berkeley: University of California Press.

Snyder, Timothy. 2003. *The Reconstruction of Nations: Poland, Ukraine, Lithuania, Belarus, 1569–1999*. New Haven: Yale University Press.

Stevenson, David. 2004. *Cataclysm: The First World War as Political Tragedy*. New York: Basic Books.

Taylor, P.J. 1993. "Geopolitical World Orders." In *Political Geography of the Twentieth Century*, ed. P.J. Taylor. New York: John Wiley & Sons.

Taylor, P.J. 1993. "Introduction: A Century of Political Geography." In *Political Geography of the Twentieth Century*, ed. P.J. Taylor. New York: John Wiley & Sons.

Trubowitz, Peter. 1998. *Defining the National Interest: Conflict and Change in American Foreign Policy*. Chicago: University of Chicago Press.

Tuchman, Barbara. 1962. *The Guns of August*. New York: Ballantine Books.

Turnock, David. 1989. *Eastern Europe: An Historical Geography 1815–1945*. London: Routledge.

U.S. Department of State. 1942. *Foreign Relations of the United States 1919: The Paris Peace Conference Vol. I*. Washington: United States Government Printing Office. (FRUS I)

U.S. Department of State. 1942. *Foreign Relations of the United States 1919: The Paris Peace Conference Vol. II*. Washington: United States Government Printing Office. (FRUS II)

U.S. Department of State. 1943. *Foreign Relations of the United States 1919: The Paris Peace Conference Vol. III*. Washington: United States Government Printing Office. (FRUS III)

U.S. Department of State. 1943. *Foreign Relations of the United States 1919: The Paris Peace Conference Vol. IV*. Washington: United States Government Printing Office. (FRUS IV)

U.S. Department of State. 1946. *Foreign Relations of the United States 1919: The Paris Peace Conference Vol. V.* Washington: United States Government Printing Office. (FRUS V)

U.S. Department of State. 1946. *Foreign Relations of the United States 1919: The Paris Peace Conference Vol. VI.* Washington: United States Government Printing Office. (FRUS VI)

U.S. Department of State. 1946. *Foreign Relations of the United States 1919: The Paris Peace Conference Vol. VII.* Washington: United States Government Printing Office. (FRUS VII)

U.S. Department of State. 1946. *Foreign Relations of the United States 1919: The Paris Peace Conference Vol. XI.* Washington: United States Government Printing Office. (FRUS XI)

U.S. Department of State. 1947. *Foreign Relations of the United States 1919: The Paris Peace Conference Vol. XII.* Washington: United States Government Printing Office. (FRUS XII)

Wallis, B.C. 1916. "Distribution of Nationalities in Hungary." *The Geographical Journal* (47:3).

Wallis, B.C. 1918 (i). "The Peoples of Austria." *Geographical Review* (6:1).

Wallis, B.C. 1918 (ii). "The Rumanians in Hungary." *Geographical Review* (6:2).

Walworth, Arthur. 1986. *Wilson and His Peacemakers: American Diplomacy at the Paris Peace Conference, 1919.* New York: W.W. Norton and Company.

Wank, Solomon. 1997. "The Hapsburg Empire." In Karen Barkey and Mark von Hagen, *After Empire: Multiethnic Societies and Nation-Building.* Boulder, CO: Westview Press.

Weigend, Guido. 1950. "Effects of Boundary Changes in the South Tyrol." *Geographical Review* (40:3).

Westermann, William. 1921. "The Armenian Problem and the Disruption of Turkey." In *What Really Happened at Paris: The Story of the Peace Conference, 1918–1919 by American Delegates*, ed. Edward House. New York: Charles Scribner's Sons.

Wilson, Woodrow. 1984. *The Papers of Woodrow Wilson, Volume 45*, edited by Arthur Link. Princeton: Princeton University Press.

White, George W. 2000. *Nationalism and Territory: Constructing Group Identity in Southeastern Europe.* Lanham, MD: Rowman & Littlefield.

White, George. 2004. *Nation, State, and Territory: Origins, Evolutions, and Relationships Volume 1.* Lanham, MD: Rowman & Littlefield.

Wood, William, and George Demko. 1999. "Political Geography for the Next Millennium." In *Reordering the World: Geopolitical Perspectives for the 21st Century* ed. William Wood and George Demko. Boulder, CO: Westview Press.

Woods, H. Charles. 1918. "Albania and the Albanians." *Geographical Review* (5:4).

Woolf, Stuart. 1996. *Nationalism in Europe, 1815 to the Present: A Reader.* London: Routledge.

PRIMARY SOURCE MATERIALS

"The Black Book," from the Isaiah Bowman Papers at the Milton S. Eisenhower Library, Johns Hopkins University, Baltimore. MS 58 Box 13.13.

Bowman, Isaiah. undated. "The Geographical Program of the American Peace Delegation, 1919," from the Isaiah Bowman Papers at the Milton S. Eisenhower Library, Johns Hopkins University, Baltimore. MS 58 Box 13.13.

Commission on Polish Affairs. *Report No. 1 of the Commission on Polish Affairs.* Paris: March 12, 1919.

Committee for the Study of Territorial Questions Relating to Rumania and Yugoslavia. *Report No. 1: Rumanian Frontiers.* Paris: April 6, 1919.

Committee for the Study of Territorial Questions Relating to Rumania and Yugoslavia. *Report No. 1: Frontiers of Yugoslavia.* Paris: April 6, 1919.

Foreign Relations of the United States 1919: The Paris Peace Conference Vols. I–XIII. Compiled by the Office of the Historian of the U.S. Department of State.

Great Britain. (Nov. 11, 1918). Parliamentary Debates (Commons), 5th Series. *Hansard.* 1917. Proceedings of the House of Commons, vol. 93. London: Government of the United Kingdom.

Miller, David Hunter. *My Diary at the Conference of Paris with Documents.* Appeal Printing Company: 1924. (40 sets produced)

"The Red Book," from the Isaiah Bowman Papers at the Milton S. Eisenhower Library, Johns Hopkins University, Baltimore. MS 58 Box 13.12.

The Treaty of St. Germain, compiled in Lawrence Martin. *The Treaties of Peace: 1919–1923 Vol. 1.* New York, Carnegie Endowment for International Peace: 1924.

The Treaty of Trianon, compiled in Lawrence Martin. *The Treaties of Peace: 1919–1923 Vol. 1.* New York, Carnegie Endowment for International Peace: 1924.

The Treaty of Versailles, compiled in Lawrence Martin. *The Treaties of Peace: 1919–1923 Vol. 1.* New York, Carnegie Endowment for International Peace: 1924.

Wilson, Woodrow. *President Wilson's Great Speeches and Other History Making Documents.* Chicago: Stanton & Van Vliet Co: 1919.

Wilson, Woodrow. *Selected Literary and Political Papers and Addresses of Woodrow Wilson: Volume II.* New York: Grosset & Dunlap: 1927.

Wilson, Woodrow. *The Papers of Woodrow Wilson, Volume 45,* edited by Arthur Link. Princeton: Princeton University Press: 1984.

Index